John Adams, William Austin

A Selection of the Patriotic Addresses, to the President of the United States

Together with the President's Answers

John Adams, William Austin

A Selection of the Patriotic Addresses, to the President of the United States
Together with the President's Answers

ISBN/EAN: 9783337192365

Printed in Europe, USA, Canada, Australia, Japan

Cover: Foto ©ninafisch / pixelio.de

More available books at **www.hansebooks.com**

A SELECTION OF THE Patriotic Addreſſes, TO THE PRESIDENT OF THE UNITED STATES.

TOGETHER WITH

The Preſident's *Anſwers.*

PRESENTED

In the year One Thouſand Seven Hundred and Ninety-Eight, and the Twenty-Second of the Independence of America.

BOSTON:

PRINTED BY JOHN W. FOLSOM,
No. 30, UNION-STREET.

1798.

DEDICATION.

TO THE

French Directory.

GENTLEMEN,

PERMIT me to address to you a work, which originated under your own hands. If there be any merit in it, if a noble spirit pervade it, if the principles of Greece and Rome, in their most illustrious days, concentre in this volume, no little glory is due to you; for you inspired them. Like fire in a flint, this volume had still been latent in the American bosom, had not your inimitable art *extracted it. While we thank you for the noble ardor which you have roused from Vermont to Georgia, we also acknowledge our obligation to you, for your fostering care of our concerns, and for your unprecedented, sincere and disinterested professions, which have arisen to such a height, that you would willingly adopt our whole nation, as your own!*

Although this volume contains a summary

of

of American, popular sentiment, on the genuineness of which you may rely; still to be ingenuous, we must confess, there are a certain few here, notorious indeed for their profession of friendship to you, but who are in reality your worst enemies. Believe me, Gentlemen, these ungrateful wretches, whom you have reared, fed and moulded to your own form and comeliness, have invariably deceived you. You have depended solely on them for information respecting us, your allies: none of them have remitted you a true statement of popular sentiment. They have abused your confidence; and nearly ruined your influence in this country. As a friend to truth, I will undeceive you, and dissipate those clouds of error in which you are involved, through the false insinuations of your agents; and this without a douceur for my service.

Rest assured, we are the same people whom you admired in time past; we are not unworthy of our ancestors; we have not deservedly lost your esteem. WARREN *was not the last of the Americans; and* WASHINGTON, *who, twenty years since, converted his spear to a pruning-hook, has lately reconverted his pruning-hook to a spear. We love peace, we confess; yet let not this, we pray you, imply an idea derogatory to our valor; we love it so ardently,*

dently, we will fight *for it. But it is the* great principle *with us, to wield the* Pen *first, if that fail, the* Sword. *Speak, sirs, if this principle be the genuine offspring of America, (and that it is, this volume carries with it, an internal evidence) are we not worthy of the esteem of the "magnanimous Republic?"*

Fully impressed with the idea, that these addresses, which I have selected *from a* vast number, *will be of great service to you in appreciating our American character, I have collected this volume, entirely for your use, and request no other favor, than, to anticipate the inference, to wit,——France! remember Britain!*

EDITOR.

P.S. Should you request a second and third volume, they shall be forwarded immediately.

THE

ADDRESSES

TO

THE PRESIDENT, &c.

VERMONT.

To the PRESIDENT *of the* UNITED STATES.

SIR,

WE, the Subſcribers, Inhabitants of the town of Windſor, in the State of Vermont, deeply impreſſed with the critical ſituation, to which our Country is reduced, by the ambitious views, ſecret intrigues and nefarious conduct of a foreign nation, aided by unprincipled and deſigning men of our own Country, conceive it our duty to declare to you our fulleſt approbation of your conduct in this arduous and important conjuncture of public affairs.

At the ſame time permit us, Sir, to aſſure you and the Congreſs of the United States, that although peace is the moſt ardent wiſh of our hearts; yet it is a peace founded upon

upon the great principles of national independence and honour, which ſhall not be degraded by the officious interference, imperious demands, or the piratical depredations of any nation on earth, and that we are ready and willing to pledge our lives and fortunes in ſupport of ſuch meaſures as the national government may think beſt to adopt to protect our commerce, defend our country from inſults, and maintain our independence and liberties inviolate.

To the INHABITANTS *of the town of* WINDSOR *in the State of* VERMONT.

GENTLEMEN,

I THANK you for this addreſs, preſented to me by your ſenators in Congreſs, Mr. Paine and Mr. Chipman.

Your attachment to peace on the principles of national independence and honor, not degraded by the officious interference, imperious demands, or piratical depredations of any nation, is amiable.

The pledges of your lives and fortunes in ſupport of ſuch meaſures, as the national government may think beſt to adopt, to protect our commerce, defend our country from

from insult and maintain our independence and liberties inviolate are honorable to you, and acceptable to your country.

JOHN ADAMS.

To JOHN ADAMS, PRESIDENT *of the* UNITED STATES.

SIR,

PERMIT the inhabitants of the towns of Arlington and Sandgate, in the county of Bennington in the state of Vermont, with the greatest respect to approach the Executive, and solemnly avow those sentiments, which for years we have cherished, and which at this time we think it criminal to suppress.

Long have we seen foreign influence prevailing, and endangering the peace and independence of our country—Long have we seen, with most painful sensations, the exertions of dangerous and restless men, misleading the understandings of our well-meaning citizens, and prompting them to such measures as would sink the glory of our country, and prostrate her liberties at the feet of France.

Long have we seen that nation departing from her precious professions of emancipa-

ting

ting the enſlaved, and following the ſteps of ambitious tyrants in the road to univerſal empire. And while we lamented that ſo many, with intemperate zeal, appeared willing to ſacrifice every thing to her glory, we charitably hoped, in times like the preſent, they would cheerfully rally around the ſtandard of government—nor are our hopes blaſted—the veil is now removed from their eyes, and the ſpell is broken. Suffer us, Sir, with perfect ſincerity, to declare that the Executive and Government of the United States have ever had our confidence. We have no attachment or excluſive friendſhip for any foreign nation. America is our country. To ſupport ſuch meaſures as our Executive and adminiſtration have or may adopt for the ſafety and defence of our national dignity and independence, we pledge ourſelves with whatever we hold dear. And while we gratefully acknowledge the goodneſs of Heaven for a conſtitution happily calculated to ſecure our ſafety and freedom, and for the wiſdom, firmneſs and juſtice with which the government of theſe United States has been adminiſtered, and which has been our ſecurity from foreign bondage, we ardently pray that the invaluable life of the Preſident may be continued, the time of his uſefulneſs protracted, his adminiſtration proſpered, and may his conduct, amid thoſe corroding cares and trying circumſtances,

circumſtances, which are inſeparable from his exalted ſtation, receive the merited acknowledgment of the preſent and of unborn generations.

To the INHABITANTS *of the Towns of* ARLINGTON *and* SANDGATE, *in the county of* BENNINGTON, *in the State of* VERMONT.

GENTLEMEN,

I THANK you for this addreſs, which has been preſented to me by Mr. Chipman, one of your ſenators in Congreſs.

Sentiments like yours, which have been entertained for years, it would be at this time, inexcuſeable not to expreſs. If you have long ſeen foreign influence prevailing, and endangering the peace and independence of our country, ſo have I; if you have long ſeen, with painful ſenſations, the exertions of dangerous and reſtleſs men, miſleading the underſtandings of our well-meaning citizens, and prompting them to ſuch meaſures, as would ſink the glory of our country, and proſtrate her liberties at the feet of France, ſo alſo have I.

I have ſeen in the conduct of the French nation, for the laſt twelve years, a repetition of their character diſplayed under Louis the ſourteenth, and little more, excepting the extravagancies,

extravagancies, which have been intermixed with it, of the wildeſt philoſophy, which was ever profeſſed in this world ſince the building of Babel, and the Fables of the Giants, who, by piling mountains on mountains, invaded the ſkies. If the ſpell is broken, let human nature exult and rejoice. The veil may be removed from the eyes of many, but I fear not of all. The ſnare is not yet entirely broken, and we are not yet eſcaped.

If you have no attachments, or excluſive friendſhip for any foreign nation, you poſſeſs the genuine character of true Americans.

The pledge of yourſelves, and deareſt enjoyments, to ſupport the meaſures of government, ſhews that your ideas are adequate to the national dignity, and that you are worthy to enjoy its independence and ſovereignty.

Your prayers for my life and uſefulneſs, are too affecting to me to be enlarged upon.

JOHN ADAMS.

To the PRESIDENT *and* CONGRESS *of the* UNITED STATES.

WE, the Mayor, Aldermen, Common Council and Freemen of the city of Vergennes, in the county of Addiſon, and ſtate of of Vermont, though deeply impreſſed with the train of lawleſs and unprovoked aggreſſions of the French nation upon our lawful commerce, the repeated inſults upon our government, the neglect and even ſtudied contempt with which our meſſengers of peace and accommodation have been treated, the general ſyſtem of policy by them adopted and perſeveringly purſued, equally deſtructive to the rights of perſons, of things and of nations, and eſpecially the dangerous influence of that policy upon the United States; yet feel a ſecurity in the wiſdom, rectitude, firmneſs and moderation of the Executive, and of Congreſs, in this eventful criſis. The official conduct of the ſupreme Executive demands the higheſt confidence of the citizens of the United States, and their moſt unequivocal expreſſions of approbation and applauſe. And we cheriſh the pleaſing hope that the united councils of the government, under the guidance of the Supreme Diſpoſer of events, will ſtill ſave us from the deſtruction with which we are ſo unjuſtly threatened. And while we expreſs our confidence in the Executive and in Congreſs, we cannot conceal our indignation at the conduct of theſe pretended patriots, whoſe ſtudies and labours (not to call in queſtion their views) are uniformly calculated to ſhackle the meaſures of adminiſtration, divide the American people from their government, and render both ſubſervient to foreign influence. But thanks to Heaven, we are not that degraded, nationleſs people, who will tamely lay our well-won glory and national happineſs in the ſcale with the barbarian demands of ſpoliators, and the inſatiable rapacity of the changeful, dependent miniſters of foreign faction.

The perfidious republic which boaſts of its *terror* and *prowеſs* to us, is more terrible in vices and impieties, than in arms: and though we wiſh to remain in the refreſhing ſhades of our fruitful vine, yet at our country's call we will cheerfully quit them to gather laurels in the rugged field of Mars. Our lives and our property, even to the laſt mite, are devoted to our country, and we freely pledge them in her cauſe, to be uſed againſt any nation on earth, which with ſacrilegious finger ſhall dare to touch the holy ark of our national rights.

To the MAYOR, ALDERMEN, COMMON COUNCIL *and* FREEMEN *of* VERGENNES, *in the County of* ADDISON, *and State of* VERMONT.

GENTLEMEN,

YOUR addreſs to the Preſident and Congreſs, has been preſented to me by your ſenators.

ſenators, Mr. Paine and Mr. Chipman, and your repreſentative, Mr. Morris,

Your oppoſition to that policy, (if indeed it can be called policy) which is equally deſtructive of perſons, things and nations, does honor to your underſtandings and diſpoſitions.

The only ſecurity we have under Heaven, is in the wiſdom, rectitude, firmneſs and moderation of Congreſs.

Your approbation of the conduct of the ſupreme executive authority of government, is very pleaſing; but you ſhould remember it can do no more than execute the laws.

If the united councils of our country can ſave us from the deſtruction with which we are ſo unjuſtly threatened, it can only be under the guidance of the Supreme Diſpoſer, by the united valor, conſtancy and exertions of the people. All who recollect the hiſtory of Vermont and its inhabitants, will eaſily underſtand them when they declare their reſolution, at the call of their country, to quit their refreſhing ſhades and fruitful vines to gather laurels in the field of Mars.

Your lives and your property will not be pledged in vain againſt the nation which, with ſacrilegious hand, ſhall touch the ark of your national rights.

JOHN ADAMS.

NEW-HAMPSHIRE.

To the PRESIDENT *of the* UNITED STATES.

SIR,

AT a time when the American nation is on the point of being drawn into the calamities of war, we flatter ourselves that an addrefs from the Legiflature of New-Hampfhire will not be unacceptable.

Permit us, Sir, to exprefs our entire fatisfaction in the wifdom and energy of your adminiftration and that of your predeceffor. Your unremitted perfeverance which has marked your endeavours to adjuft and fettle our difputes with France, difplays in the ftrongeft colours your defire of peace. Although the political fituation of this country is diftreffing and alarming, yet no meafures on your part have been wanting that could honorably render it otherwife.

We confider the inftructions given our envoys, fufficient and ample for every purpofe of honorable and equitable negociation. We feel the indignity which has been offered them—we feel with refentment the wrongs and injuries done our commerce, by French depredations.. A firm requeft and dignified demand, has not procured us redrefs: And we add, with regret, that we fear the apparent

ent diſpoſition of the government of France renders further negociation unneceſſary.

We do not tax ourſelves with ingratitude to the French nation. That debt which we contracted under the monarchy of France, we anticipated and paid to the executive government of that country; and it will always be recollected that we were the firſt nation to acknowledge the Republic of France.

It is with pleaſure we contemplate the increaſing firmneſs of our national Legiſlature. By union, our independence can be maintained; by diviſion it is loſt forever. To divide and conquer, has been (we are ſenſible) too often and ſucceſsfully practiſed to the deſtruction of governments and nations: But we are happy to aſſure you, that the oppoſition in the State of New-Hampſhire to the adminiſtration of the federal government, is much too contemptible to merit the name of diviſion.

Although we deprecate the evils and ſcourges of war; yet, Sir, we more ſenſibly feel the inſults offered the dignity of our country. Our independence was won and eſtabliſhed by the blood and fatigues of the brave. It is a boon which we will never ſacrifice at the ſhrine of foreign rapacious ambition. If declining Rome bought her peace of the ancient Gauls with money, yet we ſhall never give our conſent to pay a diſgraceful tribute to Gauls more modern.

When our country calls, our war-worn ſoldiers and the hardy youth of our hills, at the firſt ſound of the clarion of danger, will cheerfully and unitedly rally around the ſtandard of American independence, and defend it with their blood.

The diſorganizer may ſeek protection under the colours of France; but as for us and our conſtituents, we will ſhelter ourſelves under the wings of the American Eagle.

Accept, Sir, our united declaration to ſupport and defend the conſtituted authorities of our country, with our lives and fortunes.

Accept, Sir, our warmeſt wiſhes for your perſonal welfare and happineſs. Long may you continue to watch over the ſafety of the community.

To the LEGISLATURE *of* NEW-HAMPSHIRE.

GENTLEMEN,

MY moſt reſpectful and affectionate thanks are due to your two honorable Houſes for an addreſs, tranſmitted to me by your excellent governor, and preſented to me by your repreſentatives in Congreſs.

The

The American nation appears to me as it does to you, on the point of being drawn into the vortex of European war—your entire ſatisfaction in the adminiſtration of the federal government, and in the perſeverance which has marked its endeavours to adjuſt our diſputes with France, is very precious to me. Diſtreſſing and alarming as the political ſituation of this country is, I am conſcious that no meaſures on my part have been wanting that could have honorably rendered it otherwiſe. The indignities which have been ſo repeatedly offered to our ambaſſadors, the greateſt of which is the laſt unexampled inſult, in chooſing out one of the three, and diſcarding the other two, the wrongs and injuries to our commerce, by French depredations, the legal declaration, in effect, of hoſtilities againſt all our commerce, and the apparent diſpoſition of the government of France, to render further negociation not only nugatory, but diſgraceful and ruinous. You may tax the French government with ingratitude, with much more juſtice than yourſelves.

The increaſing union among the people and their legiſlatures, is as encouraging as it is agreeable. The precept "divide and conquer" was never exemplified in the eyes of mankind in ſo ſtriking and remarkable a manner as of late in Europe! Every old republic has fallen before it. If America has

has not ſpirit and ſenſe enough to learn wiſdom from the example of ſo many republican cataſtrophies paſſing in review before her eyes, ſhe deſerves to ſuffer, and moſt certainly will fall.—I am happy to aſſure you, that as far as my information extends, the oppoſition to the federal government in all the other ſtates, as well as in New-Hampſhire, is too ſmall to merit the name of diviſion; it is a difference of ſentiment on public meaſures, not an alienation of affection to their country.

The war-worn ſoldiers, and the brave and hardy ſons of New-Hampſhire, ſecond to none in ſkill, enterprize or courage in war, will never ſurrender the independence, or conſent to the diſhonour of their country.

I return my warmeſt wiſhes for your health and happineſs.

JOHN ADAMS.

To the PRESIDENT *of the* UNITED STATES.

THE ſubſcribers, inhabitants of the town of Portſmouth, State of New-Hampſhire, conceiving the preſent moment to be one of thoſe critical periods, when political neceſſity, calls aloud for the public voice to advocate the meaſures of its own government, and cheerfully to offer the ſupreme Executive,

tive, and the Congreſs of the Union, the moſt determined and unequivocal ſupport, in maintaining meaſures that have been, or may be adopted for the intereſt, honor and independence of the United States. They therefore beg leave to expreſs their high ſenſe and approbation of the wiſdom and probity which have characteriſed the various efforts of our executive, for effecting a permanent reconciliation with France; and finding that the Directory has endeavoured to impoſe ſuch terms as cannot be accepted without the vileſt proſtration of national intereſt, honor and independence. They therefore offer their property to ſupport, and their lives to defend, thoſe dear-bought, ſacred and inalienable rights; being fully reſolved to rally round the banners of their country, and follow the ſtandard of government, making every poſſible effort to convince the world, and more eſpecially the unfriendly powers of Europe, that they are not the divided people they have been repreſented to be, neither will they be the ſlaves nor dupes of any nation upon the face of the globe.

To JOHN ADAMS, PRESIDENT *of the* UNITED STATES.

AMIDST the numerous addreſſes from our fathers and brethren, throughout United America,

America, on the present critical ſituation of our country, replete with juſt indignation at the unparalleled conduct towards us, of an imperious unprincipled European power; and with aſſurances of the moſt perfect acquieſcence in, and firmeſt ſupport of every meaſure which has been, or may be, purſued by our Executive for the ſecurity of our national honor and independence: The Youth of Portſmouth, though ſenſible their ſuffrage will add comparatively little to the general maſs of patriotiſm ſo worthily diſplayed; yet impelled by a ſenſe of duty, and animated by the ſame ardent attachment to the conſtitution and laws of their country, joined to the moſt profound reſpect for its chief magiſtrate, they beg leave alſo to addreſs him on this occaſion.

Though at the commencement of our great and glorious revolution, few of us were even in exiſtence; yet have we ſince often liſtened with enthuſiaſtic rapture to the wondrous tale. With aſtoniſhment have we been told by actors in that ſublime ſcene, of the wiſdom, prudence, firmneſs, perſeverence and bravery diſplayed by the fathers and defenders of our country, in the cabinet and the field, under every diſadvantage of infancy, inexperience and poverty, againſt the moſt opulent and powerful nation on the globe, till peace, liberty and independence were obtained and eſtabliſhed on the firmeſt foundation. Theſe

These blessings having received as our birth-right, we will never part with but with life. Purchased as they were by the blood and treasure of our gallant ancestors without *our* aid: We will defend them with the last drop and particle of our own, and endeavour to prove ourselves worthy the rich inheritance.

With the justest abhorrence of the perfidy, duplicity, rapacious avarice, and daring insolence, pride and injustice of a nation who once possessed, and might still have possessed almost every American heart: We are forcibly impressed with the striking contrast of our own government, which while it secures the approbation of our seniors, excites in us the highest admiration and applause. And while we now solemnly tender our persons and lives in defence of our country, its government, laws and institutions, against all attempts to destroy, subvert or impair them; we cannot but declare that we think it a most prosperous omen, that Providence has placed at the head of government, at this alarming crisis, to defend our national honor and independence, a man, who, like his illustrious predecessor, had so large a share in procuring those invaluable blessings.

To

To the YOUNG MEN *of* PORTSMOUTH, *in the State of* NEW-HAMPSHIRE.

GENTLEMEN,

THIS handſome addreſs from the youth of Portſmouth, evinces the ſame ſpirit and principles which animate the riſing generation in general throughout the United States, and is not leſs agreeable to me than any I have before received.

The opinion you have formed of the wiſdom, prudence, firmneſs, perſeverance and bravery of your fathers, is not exaggerated, and their example is worthy of your imitation. They have another merit, which I may recollect with propriety ;—they have educated their ſons in their own principles, and inſpired into them their own virtues ; a fact which is every day more and more apparent, and forms the ſureſt foundation of hope and confidence for our country.

Nothing can be more flattering to my heart, than the confidence in me, manifeſted by you, and your contemporaries, through the Union in general—may it never be diſappointed.

JOHN ADAMS.

From

From the STUDENTS *of* DARTMOUTH UNIVERSITY, *to* JOHN ADAMS, PRESIDENT *of the* UNITED STATES.

SIR,

GROWING up from our cradles in a land of liberty, and taught, by precept and experience, to value the bleſſings of a free government, we feel an indignation at any attempt to ſtain its honor, or trouble its peace.

We are young, without experience; it therefore becomes us to be diffident in regard to meaſures of political practice. But when the rulers of a foreign nation are endeavouring to proſtrate our liberties; are flattering themſelves that the people of theſe ſtates are taking a part ſeparate from the government, and in this deluſion are calculating their influence over us; while men of different profeſſions and ages, from various parts of our land, are expreſſing their approbation of the meaſures of government;—we ſolicit that you would accept a tribute of duty and reſpect from us, a band of youth, members of a ſeat of ſcience, in the northern region of an extenſive republic; and that you would be aſſured of our love, our attachment, our confidence in your adminiſtration, and the legiſlative bodies, in regard to our foreign as well as domeſtic intereſts.

C If,

If, notwithſtanding the meaſures which have been wiſely propoſed, and prudently applied and executed, for accommodating difficulties with the French, that nation ſhould ſtill continue in the ſpirit of domination and practice of abuſes towards us; if our government ſhould think it neceſſary to change the ſcene of negociation from the cabinet to the field of battle; we offer our zeal, our activity and our lives, to repel the foe that would make us ſlaves.

At your command, illuſtrious magiſtrate of a great people, we will haſten to the ſtandard of freemen and warriors.

To the STUDENTS *of* DARTMOUTH UNIVERSITY, *in the State of* NEW-HAMPSHIRE.

GENTLEMEN,

I THANK you for this addreſs, preſented to me by Mr. Freeman, your repreſentative in Congreſs.

Your modeſt diffidence, in regard to meaſures of political practice, well becomes your age, and the purſuits of ſcience and literature, which have, as they ought, occupied hitherto, the moſt of your time; but it behoves you to conſider well the ſituation of your country, at the time you are to enter on the ſtage of life, and prepare yourſelves for the part you muſt act.

Be

Be assured, that your tribute of duty and respect, your love, attachment and confidence, are words of precious import which cannot be considered by me as words of course, nor as words of art.

The offer of your zeal, activity and lives, to repel the foe that would make us slaves, in case your government should determine it necessary to change the scene of negociation for the field of battle, is very amiable and affecting. You cannot all be soldiers; society must be supplied with the ordinary professions and faculties, in time of war, as well as in peace. Those of you who feel an inclination to a life of danger and glory, may find employment for all the activity and enterprize of your genius in due time.

Let me intreat you, and all my young friends in America, whether students or men of business, not to be dazzled by the splendor, or intimidated by the horror of modern events. Remember that the Roman republic was revived in the fourteenth century, that Rienzi was as famous as the modern heroes—Petrarch was his friend and admirer—that atheism and blasphemy were as prevalent and fashionable then as they are now, at least in Italy. Let not a young country, and the only really growing empire in the world, be corrupted and ruined by such extravagancies.

JOHN ADAMS.

MASSACHUSETTS.

To the PRESIDENT *of the* UNITED STATES.

SIR,

THE Legiſlature of Maſſachuſetts, ever anxious and long habituated to take an early and decided part in whatever relates to the ſafety and welfare of their country, beg leave to join the united voice of your fellow citizens, in offering you a teſtimony of their reſpect and confidence.

As a native citizen of our commonwealth, and as the ſupreme Executive of the government of our deliberate choice, we feel for you thoſe ſentiments of attachment and veneration, which the recollection of your long, diſtinguiſhed and ſucceſsful ſervices are calculated to excite;—and if the meaſures of a wiſe and virtuous adminiſtration, ſuch as we believe your's to have been, can receive aid or ſanction from our moſt decided and unequivocal approbation, our duty in expreſſing it will be diſcharged with increaſed ſatisfaction.

It is with a mixture of indignation and regret, that we learn the ſtate of our negociations with the French republic. From a careful review of our relations with France, and of the unremitting efforts of the national government, to preferve and perpetuate her friendfhip, we might readily have believed that there could be no crifis in the progrefs of her political career, in which our tranquillity could have been difturbed. But amidft the collifion of parties, France has loft the object of her revolution. She once fought for liberty,—fhe now contends for dominion; and having declared by the voice of her executive, that "fhe ought to become the model and the arbiter of nations," has violated the rights of every neutral people, and proftrated the governments of moft of the republics of Europe.

Should any further attempts, either to controul the government, or fubjugate the people of the United States, be the refult of her inordinate ambition, the citizens of Maffachufetts will meet them with the firm and determined fpirit of freemen; and as they have been among the firft to defend, will be the laft to refign the rights of national fovereignty.

In this all-important conflict, we expect the ready and zealous co-operation of the free and enlightened people of America: and our country, having adopted every reafonable meafure to avert the calamities of war, may, with humble confidence, rely upon the God of our fathers, for protection and fuccefs.

A people, by whom the bleſſings of civil and religious liberty are enjoyed and duly appreciated, will never ſurrender them but with their lives. We will never forget that our charter to this liberty is ſealed with the blood of Americans. And we pledge to you the patriotiſm and all the energies of our conſtituents, that it ſhall never be violated by the ſacrilegious hand of foreign power. We alſo moſt ſolemnly pledge ourſelves, to ſupport every meaſure, which the government of the United States, at this momentous period may ſee ſit to adopt, to protect the commerce, and preſerve the independence of our country.

To the LEGISLATURE *of* MASSACHUSETTS.

GENTLEMEN,

AN affectionate and reſpectful addreſs from your two honorable Houſes, has been preſented to me, according to your requeſt, by your ſenators and repreſentatives in Congreſs.

The anxiety, the ancient and conſtant habit of the people of Maſſachuſetts and their legiſlature to take an early and decided

The first forty years of my life were passed in my native Massachusetts, in a course of education and professional career, which led me to a very general acquaintance in every part of that state. If with your opportunities, and pressing motives for observation, and experience, you can pronounce my services successful and administration virtuous, and the people of fifteen other states could concur with you in that opinion, my reward would be complete, and my most ardent wishes gratified.

If the object of France, in her revolution, ever was liberty, it was a liberty very ill defined and never understood. She now aims at dominion such as never has before prevailed in Europe. If with the principles, maxims and systems of her present leaders, she is to become the model and arbiter of nations, the liberties of the world will be in danger. Nevertheless, the citizens of Massachusetts, who were first to defend, will be among the last to resign the rights of our national sovereignty.

You have great reason to expect, in this all-important conflict, the ready and zealous co-operation of the free and enlightened people of America, and with humble confidence to rely on the God of our fathers for protection and success.

With

With you I fully agree, that a people by whom the bleſſings of civil and religious liberty are enjoyed, and duly appreciated, will never ſurrender them but with their lives. The patriotiſm and the energies of your conſtituents, united with thoſe of the people of the other ſtates, are a ſure pledge, that the charter of your civil and religious liberties ſealed by the blood of Americans, will never be violated by the ſacrilegious hand of foreign power.

The ſolemn pledge of yourſelves to ſupport every meaſure which the government of the United States, at this momentous period, may ſee fit to adopt to protect the commerce and preſerve the independence of our country, muſt afford an important encouragement to the national government, and contribute greatly to the union of the people throughout all the ſtates.

JOHN ADAMS.

To JOHN ADAMS, PRESIDENT, *and to the* CONGRESS *of the* UNITED STATES.

THE ſubſcribers, inhabitants and citizens of Boſton, in the State of Maſſachuſetts, deeply impreſſed with the critical and alarming ſituation of the United States;—and convinced of the neceſſity of unanimity and firmneſs at this intereſting moment, beg leave

to

to expreſs to the ſupreme Executive, and the Congreſs of the United States, their fulleſt approbation of the meaſures adopted by the Preſident, relative to our foreign relations, their gratitude for his exertions to conciliate the French republic, and his ſolicitude to ſettle and accommodate all exiſting differences, upon terms compatible with the ſafety, the intereſt, and the dignity of the United States.

They beg leave alſo to expreſs their high and elevated opinion of, and confidence in, the virtue, the wiſdom, and the prudence of the national government, and their fixed reſolution to ſupport, at the riſk of their lives and fortunes, ſuch meaſures as the Preſident and Congreſs, in their wiſdom ſhall determine to be neceſſary to promote and ſecure the honor and happineſs of the United States;—Nor can they omit, at this criſis, and upon ſuch an occaſion, to declare to the world, that they are not humiliated under a colonial ſenſe of fear;—"they are not a divided people:" that they know their rights, and are determined to ſupport them.

To the INHABITANTS *and* CITIZENS *of* BOSTON.

GENTLEMEN,

I THANK you for the declaration of your approbation of the meaſures adopted by by me, relative to our foreign relations, to conciliate the French republic, and to accommodate all exifting difference, upon terms compatible with the fafety, the intereft, and the dignity of the United States.

Your high and elevated opinion of, and confidence in the virtue, wifdom and patriotifm, of the national government, and fixed refolution to fupport at the rifk of your lives and fortunes, fuch meafures as may be determined to be neceffary to promote and fecure, the honor and happinefs of the United States, do you honor, and are perfectly in character.

It muft, however, be a very unnatural, and peculiar ftate of things, to make it neceffary, or proper, in you, or any other American in your behalf, to declare to the world, what the world ought to have known and acknowledged without hefitation—that you are not humiliated under a colonial fenfe of fear,—that you are not a divided people, in any point which involves the honor, fafety, and effential rights of your country,—that you know your rights, and are determined to fupport them.

JOHN ADAMS.

To

To JOHN ADAMS, PRESIDENT *of the* UNITED STATES.

AT a period, when a powerful and perfidious nation, aspiring to the domination of the world, annuls in the career of her pride, all bonds of national amity; when the most conciliating measures which the pacific disposition of our government has adopted, have been repelled with indignity, silence would become cowardice, and neutrality treason.

At this eventful crisis, the Young Men of Boston, solemnly impressed with the ideas of independence, which they have derived from their ancestors, in that unequivocal language which admits of no adulation, beg leave to express to the first magistrate of the Union, their sentiments and resolutions.

Ushered into life at a time when our fathers were struggling for the rights to which God and nature entitled them, we date our existence coeval with the independence of our country. With our first breath we imbibed a detestation of servility to any nation, and we have not yet learned to submit to the humiliation of foreign controul.

As Americans, we feel an enthusiasm in applauding your arduous administration, together with that of your illustrious predecessor, ever designated by the firmest virtue, which

which danger has not been able to appal, and obloquy has in vain aſſailed. While we have admired the dignified moderation, which has marked the ſucceſſive attempts at a reconciliation with our Gallic allies, we have witneſſed with regret our proffered terms of adjuſtment, contemptuouſly rejected by the rapacity of avarice, and the inſolence of power. The inſulting demands by which France has ſo glaringly developed her punic faith, and her inſidious deſigns, we conceive would be more characteriſtic of the deſpotic requiſitions of a conqueror, than of propoſals to a high ſpirited, and we believe, an unconquerable people.

Although we preſume not to arrogate to ourſelves the office of judging on intricate queſtions of politics, yet where gratitude claims the tribute, we muſt feelingly eulogize the unſullied patriotiſm and uniform wiſdom of our ſupreme Executive.

Juſtly appreciating the ſweets of peace and the reign of equal laws, ſpurning acquieſcence to any preſumptuous power to the degradation of national honor, and determined to guard the inviolability of our conſtitution, as the palladium of our rights, we the youth of Boſton, united by indiſſoluble ties in one common love to our country, moſt ſolemnly offer, when its voice demands the energy of action, to ſacrifice our youth-

ful

ful profpects and our lives, in unnerving the arm of fedition, and repelling the inroads of oppreffion; fervently according in thofe noble fentiments, that "neutrality ought never to be purchafed by the violation of public faith, the tarnifhing of moral character, or the abandonment of independence."

To the YOUNG MEN *of* BOSTON.

GENTLEMEN,

IT is impoffible for you to enter your own Faneuil-Hall, or to throw your eyes on the variegated mountains, and elegant iflands around you, without recollecting the principles and actions of your fathers, and feeling what is due to their example:—One of their firft principles was to unite in themfelves the character of citizens and foldiers, and efpecially to preferve the latter always fubordinate to the former.

With much folicitude for your welfare, and that of your pofterity, I take the freedom to fay, that this country never appeared to me to be in greater danger, than at this moment, from within or without—never more urgently excited, to affume the functions of foldiers.

The ftate of the world is fuch, the fituation of all the nations of Europe, with which we have relation, is fo critical, that viciffitudes must be expected, from whose deleterious influences, nothing but arms and energy can protect us :—To arms, then, my young friends,—to arms, especially by sea, to be used as the laws shall direct, let us resort ; for safety against dangers, which we now see and feel, cannot be averted by truth, reason, or justice.

Nothing in the earlier part of my public life, animated me more, than the countenances of the children and youth of the town of Boston ; and nothing at this hour, gives me so much pleasure, as the masculine temper and talents, displayed by the youth of America, in every part of it.

I ought not forget the worst enemy we have ;—That obloquy, which you have observed, is the worst enemy to virtue, and the best friend to vice ; it strives to destroy all distinction between right and wrong, it leads to divisions, sedition, civil war, and military despotism.—I need say no more.

JOHN ADAMS.

To the PRESIDENT *and* CONGRESS *of the* UNITED STATES *of* AMERICA.

PENETRATED with a lively conviction of the critical and very interesting situation of of our national concerns, the ſubſcribers, inhabitants of the town of Salem, in the Commonwealth of Maſſachuſetts, are induced to preſent the following addreſs.

Senſible we are of the impropriety of an interference from the people with the eſtabliſhed adminiſtration of government, ſtill we conceive occaſions may ariſe, when an expreſſion of the public ſentiment may be highly important and beneficial. As ſuch an one we view the preſent; when the leaders of a great nation are inflexibly purſuing the moſt injurious and baneful deſigns againſt us; and flattering themſelves with a proſpect of ſucceſs, by a ſeparation of the people from the government.

It is our diſpoſition, and, as far as our influence may extend, it ſhall be our endeavour, to diſappoint and fruſtrate theſe expectations.

We are fully ſatisfied with the meaſures taken by the ſupreme Executive, for accommodating the differences ſubſiſting between the United States and the French republic; and it is with ſincere regret we learn that thoſe meaſures have been unſucceſsful.

We ſtill wiſh for peace, and a reſtoration of harmony, with that republic. But ſhould they remain implacable; ſhould we be driven to extremities; depending ſupremely on the patronage of the Moſt High, we repoſe firm confidence in the wisdom and fidelity of our rulers, with the steady patriotism and combined exertions of our fellow citizens, for maintaining a vigorous defence. We are determined, at every hazard, to support the government of our choice: and to those, to whom the powers of government are entrusted, we will afford our hearty concurrence and aid, for carrying into effect such measures as they may see fit to adopt; holding in the highest estimation our rights and interests as a free and independent people—those rights and interests for which we have once contended, and which it is our settled purpose never to resign.

To the INHABITANTS *of the Town of* SALEM, *in the State of* MASSACHUSETTS.

GENTLEMEN,

THIS address, subscribed with such unanimity by the inhabitants of your most ancient town, whose simplicity, economy, industry, enterprize, intelligence, and consequent independence and opulence, form a model deserving the imitation of all your commercial fellow-citizens, ought to have great weight, wherever it appears.

The interference of the people, by respectful expressions of their sense to the legislature, (at all times their right) cannot be denied

denied to be expedient at ſuch a time as this, when the leaders of a great nation are inflexibly purſuing the moſt injurious and baneful deſigns againſt us, and flattering themſelves with a proſpect of ſucceſs, by a ſeparation of the people from the government. Of your diſpoſition and endeavours to diſappoint theſe expectations, no man, who knows you, will doubt.

Your ſatisfaction with the meaſures of the Executive is very grateful to me; and your ſupreme dependence on the patronage of the Moſt High—the firm confidence you repoſe in the wiſdom and fidelity of our rulers, with the ſteady patriotiſm, and combined exertions, of our fellow citizens, for maintaining a vigorous defence—I truſt will not be diſappointed.

The determination, at every hazard, to ſupport the government of your choice, and the high eſtimation in which you hold your rights, as a free, independent people, for which you have once contended, and which it is your ſettled purpoſe never to reſign, are worthy of your characters, and will be fully credited by all the world.

JOHN ADAMS.

To the PRESIDENT *of the* UNITED STATES.

SIR,

THE inhabitants of the town of Newbury-Port, fully impreſſed with the preſent important criſis of public affairs, are prompted no leſs by a ſenſe of duty than by their own feelings, to expreſs thoſe ſentiments, which the occaſion ſo naturally inſpires in the breaſt of every American. From the long experience of your conduct in the many public offices to which you have been called by your own country, they feel the moſt perfect confidence in your wiſdom, integrity and patriotiſm; and they with cheerfulneſs declare their entire approbation of your attempt to adjuſt all exiſting diſputes with the French republic, by an amicable negociation; of that ſpirit of conciliation which dictated your inſtructions to our miniſters; and of the principles of juſtice on which they were founded. They learn with equal indignation and aſtoniſhment, that this ſpirit of conciliation has been repelled with contempt, that theſe principles of juſtice have been diſregarded, and that a heavy tribute, with humiliating conceſſions on our part, have been propoſed to us in a manner arbitrary and unfriendly, as the price at which we muſt purchaſe the right of being heard. The inhabitants of this town duly appreciate the bleſſings of peace and neutrality; but they will never complain at the loſs of thoſe bleſſings, when conſtrained to ſacrifice them to the honor, the dignity, and the eſſential intereſts of their country. They conſider the preſent intereſting ſtate of public affairs as a ſolemn appeal to the hearts of all independent Americans, and a call on them to come forward with unanimity and firmneſs, in ſupport of the government, and of the men of their choice—to reſiſt with becoming dignity any vain attempt to derogate from our common ſovereignty, or to dedegrade our national character from the rank it now juſtly holds among nations—to convince the world that we are alike, uninfluenced by corruption and by fear—and that, we will not be a divided people, the miſerable ſlaves of a foreign power, or the deſpicable tools of foreign influence.

Impreſſed with theſe ſentiments, and relying with full confidence on the wiſdom and patriotiſm of every branch of government, they take this occaſion ſolemnly to pledge their lives and fortunes to ſupport the meaſures judged neceſſary by the Preſident and Congreſs, to preſerve and ſecure the happineſs, the dignity, and the eſſential intereſt of the United States.

To the INHABITANTS of NEWBURY-PORT.

GENTLEMEN,

THE addrefs of the inhabitants of the ancient, populous and wealthy town of Newbury-Port, paffed without a diffentient voice at a late meeting, as certified by your felectmen, and prefented to me by your reprefentative in Congrefs, Mr. Bartlet, does me great honor.

The aftonifhment and indignation you exprefs at the contempt with which a fpirit of conciliation has been repelled, your refolution never to complain at the lofs of the bleffings of peace and neutrality, when conftrained to facrifice them to the honor, dignity and effential intereft of your country; to refift with becoming dignity any vain attempt to derogate from our common fovereignty, or to degrade our national character from the rank it now juftly holds among nations, to convince the world that you are alike uninfluenced by corruption and by fear, that you are not a divided people, the miferable flaves of foreign influence---do equal honor to your hearts and judgment.

Your reliance, with full confidence on the wifdom and patriotifm of every branch of the government, and the folemn pledge of your lives and fortunes to fupport the meafures of the legiflature and adminiftration,

to

to preserve and secure the happiness, dignity and essential interest of the United States; are all the assurances which the best of governments could desire from the best of citizens.

JOHN ADAMS.

To JOHN ADAMS, President of the United States.

SIR,

THE Grand Jurors for the county of Plymouth, in the Commonwealth of Massachusetts, attending at the Supreme Judicial Court for said county, have been led by their own reflections on the course of events, and by the excellent and impressive observations of the chief Justice in his charge at the opening of the court, to contemplate the political situation of our country—Many of us have found it difficult to believe, that a nation avowedly struggling for liberty and independence, should attempt to invade or impair those blessings where they are quietly and fully enjoyed. But the experience of several of the last years of our history, has convinced us of our mistake. While occupied in our peaceful labours, we have seen the fruits of those labours plundered and condemned, on frivolous and groundless pretences, by professed friends. Our tranquility has been disturbed by incessant appeals

peals to the paſſions of the people, by factious and deſigning men; and by repeated and audacious attempts to ſeparate the people from the government;—our ſincere deſire for peace has been met with neglect or contempt; and odious and extravagant demands, dictated by rapacity and a thirſt for boundleſs rule, have been made the terms of negociation. In ſuch a criſis, when all that is dear and valuable to freemen, when liberty and independence, national honor, ſocial order, and public ſafety appear to be in danger—a danger which union alone, under the bleſſing of heaven, can repel: We think it not improper to ſtep aſide from the ordinary duties of our office, and to expreſs to you our grateful acknowledgments for the firmneſs and diſcretion with which you have encountered ſuch new and peculiar difficulties. We are aſſured that all the energies of our common country, will aid you in ſuch a cauſe.

We pray the God of all intelligence to preſerve the force of your mind unabated, and in any arduous iſſue, to which the arts or arms of ſucceſsful violence may compel us, we pledge ourſelves "as become faithful citizens of this happy country, as one man, to come forward in the defence of all that is dear to us."

To the GRAND JURY, *for the County of* PLYMOUTH, *in the State of* MASSACHUSETTS.

GENTLEMEN,

I THANK you for your addrefs, which has been tranfmitted to me, according to your requeft, by the chief Juftice of the ftate.

Difficult as it is to believe that a nation ftruggling or pretending to ftruggle for liberty and independence, fhould attempt to invade or impair thofe bleffings, where they are quietly and fully enjoyed; yet thus it is, that the United States of America are not the only example of it.

While occupied in your peaceful employments, you have feen the fruits of your induftry plundered by profeffed friends, your tranquillity has been difturbed, by inceffant appeals to the paffions and prejudices of the people, by defigning men, and by audacious attempts to feparate the people from the government—and there is not a village in the United States perhaps, which cannot teftify to fimilar abufes.

Liberty, independence, national honor, focial order and public fafety, appear to you to be in danger; your acknowledgments to me, therefore, are the more obliging and encouraging.

Your

Your prayers for my preſervation, and your pledge that in any arduous iſſue, to which the arts or arms of ſucceſsful violence may compel us, you will, as becomes faithful citizens of this happy country, come forward as one man, in defence of all that is dear to us, are to me as affecting, as to the public they ought to be ſatisfactory ſentiments—the more affecting to me, as they come from the moſt ancient ſettlement, in the northern part of the continent, held in peculiar veneration by me at all times.

JOHN ADAMS.

To the PRESIDENT *of the* UNITED STATES.

SIR,

WHEN we contemplate the wiſdom and firmneſs, the integrity and magnanimity of our national Executive, we rejoice that we are men, we boaſt that we are Americans!

When Britain treated America with more than ſtepdame cruelty, the daring infant manfully aſſerted her rights, and bade defiance to her foe. A ſurviving few of us acted on the memorable 19th of April—we ſaw unſheathed the firſt conquering ſword—Concord drank the firſt blood of martyred freemen---here commenced a conteſt, dubious for Columbia; but by the perilous patriotiſm

triotiſm of her ſons, and the all-conquering ſword of God and Waſhington, ſhe won her ſovereign independence, and founded a growing empire on the indeſtructible baſis of juſtice and equal rights.

We, Sir, having kept a watchful eye on your active merit, from the firſt dawn of your political exiſtence, until you roſe to the *acme* of political greatneſs, recognize with warmeſt gratitude your ſignal ſervices, during the tempeſt of a revolution, which challenges obliterating time to blot it from the ſcroll of fame. We revere your inviolable attachment to the intereſts of our country, which ſhone with eclat, in framing and defending our immortal conſtitution, which exhibits wiſdom, inferior only to divine.

While we view with fulleſt ſatisfaction, peerleſs Waſhington's equitable adminiſtration, we cordially acquieſce, in the unſhaken rectitude, the amicable diſpoſition, and the vigorous meaſures now adopted by our Executive towards an aſpiring power, who, unprovoked, has outraged the piracy and perfidy of Gothic darkneſs and Vandal barbarity; who has perpetrated crimes unparalleled in the hiſtory of man! France, graſping at univerſal domination, has abandoned every moral and religious principle; trampled on ſacred faith, ſported with national laws, and demanded pecuniary exactions, which would bankrupt our nation, and render us slaves, instead of a free, sovereign and independent people. Shall we submit to these repeated insults, and humiliating demands, or resolve, in holy remembrance of those who bled, that we will defend by our valor, what they won by their blood? We would not dictate, but should the crisis demand, we will rally round the standard of our government, and under the direction of the concentrated wisdom of the union, make a free-will offering of our lives and fortunes, sooner than truckle to the mandates of any foreign power. We will gloriously perish in the attempt; or unsullied, transmit to posterity, what we received in early days, from those who are now transmitted to brighter worlds, or trembling beneath the weight of age.

We, in unison with the Union, will convince France and the world, that the divine enthusiasm of '75, glows in the bosom of each genuine American, and under Providence, will render Columbia as formidable to her foes, as was Michael's sword from the the armoury of God, to the rebel angels of Heaven!

To the INHABITANTS *of* CONCORD *in* MASSACHUSETTS.

GENTLEMEN,

I THANK you for this addreſs. Your encomium on the Executive authority of the national government, is in a degree highly flattering.

As I have ever wiſhed to avoid, as far as prudence and neceſſity would permit, every concealment from my fellow citizens, of my real ſentiments, in matters of importance, I will venture to aſk you whether it is conſiſtent with the peace we have made, the friendſhip we have ſtipulated, or even with civility, to expreſs a marked reſentment to a foreign power who is at war with another, whoſe ill will we experience every day, and who will, very probably, in a few weeks, be acknowledged an enemy in the ſenſe of the law of nations? A power, too, which invariably acknowledged us to be a nation for fifteen years; a power that has never had the inſolence to reject your ambaſſadors; a power that at preſent convoys your trade and their own at the ſame time. Immortal hatred, inextinguiſhable animoſity, is neither philoſophy, true religion, nor good policy. Our ancient maxim was, "Enemies in war, in peace friends."

If Concord drank the firſt blood of martyred freemen, Concord ſhould be the firſt to forget the injury, when it is no longer useful to remember it. Some of you, as well as myself, remember the war of 1755, as well as that of 1775. War always has its horrors, and civil wars the worst.

If the contest you allude to was dubious, it was from extrinsic causes; it was from partial, enthusiastic and habitual attachment to a foreign country---not from any question of a party of strength. It is highly useful to reflect---50,000 men upon paper, and 30,000 men in fact, was the highest number Britain ever had in arms in this country---compute the tonnage of ships necessary and actually employed, to transport these troops across the Atlantic; What were 30,000 men to the United States of America, in 1775? What would 60,000 be now in 1798?

Let not fond attachments, enthusiastic devotion, to another power, paralize the nerves of our citizens a second time, and all the ships in Europe that can be spared, officered and manned, will not be sufficient to bring to this country an army capable of any long contest.

Your compliments to me are far beyond my merits: Your confidence in the government, and determination to support it, are greatly to your honor.

JOHN ADAMS.

From

From the INHABITANTS *of the Town of* HAVERHILL, *in* MASSACHUSETTS, *to the* PRESIDENT *of the* UNITED STATES.

SIR,

WHILE we difapprove an interference of the people with the adminiftration of our national government, we confider it our duty, at this time, to affure you that the meafures you have adopted and purfued, as firft magiftrate of the Union, have uniformly met our hearty concurrence.

In full confidence that thofe meafures have been dictated by wifdom and the pureft principles of patriotifm, we cannot withhold the expreffion of our grateful thanks for your undeviating firmnefs in their execution.

Your late exertions to redrefs our wrongs, to accommodate differences unhappily exifting between this country and the French republic, to conciliate the affections of our allies, to preferve our neutrality, to eftablifh our peace and happinefs, and above all, to fupport the independence, dignity and freedom of the United States, afford the higheft evidence of the juftice and wifdom of your adminiftration; and demand, in an eminent degree, the gratitude of every patriotic American.

We humbly deprecate the calamities of war; but when the fafety, the independence, the freedom of our country require--Under the direction of the government of our choice, imploring the blessings of heaven, we are prepared with our property, and at the hazard of our lives, to support our government, to vindicate our rights, and to defend our country.

To the INHABITANTS *of the Town of* HAVERHILL, *in the State of* MASSACHUSETTS.

GENTLEMEN,

I THANK you for a respectful and affectionate address, which has been presented to me by Mr. Bartlett, your representative in Congress.

The interference of the people with the administration of the national government, in ordinary cases, would be not only useless and unnecessary, but very inconvenient and expensive to them, if not calculated to disturb the public councils with prejudices, passions, local views, and partial interests which would better be at rest; but there are some great conjunctures in which it is proper, and in such a government as ours, perhaps necessary. If ever such an occasion can occur, the present is one.

Your assurance to me that the measures I have adopted, as first magistrate of the Union, have uniformly met your hearty concurrence, and your declaration that you are prepared with your property, and at the hazard

ard of your lives, to support your government, vindicate your rights and defend your country, are to me great consolation.

JOHN ADAMS.

To the PRESIDENT *and* CONGRESS *of the* UNITED STATES.

AT a crisis in which the dignity and independence of the United States is at stake---at a moment when an union of sentiment is necessary to be evinced---

The subscribers, inhabitants and citizens of the town of Gloucester, in the Commonwealth of Massachusetts, cannot fail of expressing their fullest approbation of the wise and magnanimous conduct of the President of the United States, relative to our foreign relations, more particularly for the measures adopted by him for the honorable adjustment of any existing difficulties between the French republic and this country, and his instructions to our envoys to effect this desirable purpose: Nor can they refrain from declaring their utmost confidence in the virtue, wisdom and prudence of the national government.

And while they deprecate the evils of war, should so unhappy an event take place, (which may God in his infinite mercy avert) ---They

---They moſt ſacredly avow their determination to ſupport the conſtitution, and at the riſk of their lives and fortunes to preſerve inviolate, the rights and liberties of their country.

To the President and Congress of the United States.

AT this important criſis, we the ſubſcribers, citizens of Roxbury, in the Commonwealth of Maſſachuſetts, in order to convince the world, as far as lies within our power, that the citizens of theſe ſtates, are not a people ſeparated from their government; but firmly attached to its intereſts; at the ſame time impreſſed with the fulleſt conviction, of the purity of their intention, as well as the ability and wiſdom of their adminiſtration, feel it our duty to declare in this explicit manner, an approbation of their conduct, and determination to ſupport, with our lives and fortunes, ſuch meaſures as they ſhall determine moſt conducive to the ſafety and proſperity of the nation.

In the convulſions of Europe, it is moſt devoutly to be wiſhed, that America may not be involved:---That the freeſt, and moſt peaceable government in the world, may exerciſe its internal concerns, without any external

external controul or influence :---That no tribute or arbitrary exactions may ever be imperiously demanded ; and that the price of peace may never be national degradation. With these sentiments, we beg leave to assure the whole government, that we will readily, and cheerfully co-operate in such measures, as our own authorities, lawfully constituted, shall deem necessary, to preserve the union, and support the independence of of the United States of America.

To the CITIZENS of ROXBURY, in the State of MASSACHUSETTS.

GENTLEMEN,

A RESPECTFUL address, to the President and Congress of the United States, subscribed by one hundred and thirty-four citizens of Roxbury, has been presented to me, by Mr. Otis, your representative in Congress.

Your testimony to the purity of the intentions, as well as to the ability and wisdom of the administration ; your approbation of their conduct, and determination to support with your lives and fortunes, such measures as they shall determine most conducive to the safety, and prosperity of the nation, are peculiarly agreeable to me.

It

It is indeed devoutly to be wiſhed, that in the convulſions of Europe, America might not be involved---but the wiſhes, and prayers of the beſt of men, and moſt virtuous nations for peace, are not always heard ---the wiſhes of America have been ſo obviouſly juſt and reaſonable, that all the powers of Europe, appear to have ſhewn them ſome reſpect, excepting one, which ſeems to have left us no alternative.

JOHN ADAMS.

To the PRESIDENT *of the* UNITED STATES *of* AMERICA.

SIR,

FULLY impreſſed with a ſenſe of the importance of confiding in rulers of our own choice, eſpecially when they have been long employed, and often times in the moſt trying circumſtances, in the ſervice of their country, and have ever been found faithful to its intereſts: We the ſubſcribers, inhabitants of the town of Cambridge, take the liberty at this important criſis of our public affairs, of expreſſing our high ſatisfaction in your adminiſtration.

The part you have frequently had to act in your various important and highly reſponſible public employments, has ſometimes been attended with great difficulties and

and embarraſſments; but you have ever diſcharged your duty with diſtinguiſhed honor to yourſelf and advantage to theſe ſtates. We are perſuaded, Sir, that your ſituation could never have been more difficult and trying, than ſince you have been in your preſent office, eſpecially as it has reſpected our diſpute with France; but with pleaſure we perceive from your late communications to Congreſs, that your whole conduct in this buſineſs has been marked with the higheſt wiſdom, and that you have done every thing on your part, by the moſt prudent and conciliating meaſures to ſettle all differences between this country and that republic, upon principles of equity; while with juſt indignation we diſcover in the French government, a conduct directly the reverſe, and requiſitions, merely preparatory to negotiation, which, if complied with, would place us in the loweſt ſtate of degradation, and render us unworthy the character of a free, ſovereign and independent nation. We have the firmeſt confidence, that the meaſures of our national government will continue to be marked, under your adminiſtration, with that integrity, wiſdom and firmneſs which have diſtinguiſhed it from its firſt eſtabliſhment, and we truſt, under Providence, will prove its impregnable defence.

Although we lament, Sir, the occaſion, which ſeemed to require a diſcloſure of your inſtructions

inſtructions to the American envoys, and of their communications; yet we rejoice moſt ſincerely in its happy effect upon the public mind, which has been thereby awakened, enlightened and ſtrengthened. This good effect is conſpicuous in many of the inhabitants of this town, whoſe late reſolves, memorial and addreſs, implicitly criminating the views and adminiſtration of the ſupreme Executive, were prematurely and inconſiderately adopted from partial and erroneous conceptions, and an honeſt, but miſguided attachment to the French nation and government. While we offer this apology for thoſe haſty proceedings, we cannot but expreſs our unqualified diſapprobation of them, as unfounded, improper, and highly injurious to the Preſident of the Union.

The intrigues of the French rulers, and the principles upon which they have for a long time acted, of revolutionizing governments, even republics, with which they have no right to interfere, we abhor and will firmly oppoſe. We wiſh not their aid to teach us the principles of national liberty or law to govern ourſelves. As we will not tamely become tributary to gratify their avaricious and deſpotic views; ſo we revolt at the idea of ſuffering them to model our governments, or to dictate to us the perſons who ſhall adminiſter them.

Knowing

Knowing and feeling ourſelves to be free and happy under our preſent government, we believe any change would be for the worſe. Around the ſtandard of our own government only will we rally; and we ſolemnly renew our obligations, and pledge ourſelves to defend it to the utmoſt of our abilities, againſt domeſtic faction, and foreign influence or invaſion, as againſt "the peſtilence that walketh in darkneſs, and the deſtruction which waſteth at noonday."

Accept, Sir, our cordial congratulations on the preſent more favorable aſpect of our national concerns. We hope that none will continue to aſſert, that the people of theſe ſtates are ſeparate from, and at enmity with their government; and we truſt that the union, which ſo happily ſubſiſts among the citizens at large, will be followed by a perfect harmony in our public councils, in all meaſures requiſite to a complete vindication and ſupport of our dignity and intereſts, as a free, ſovereign, and independent nation.

To the INHABITANTS *of the Town of* CAMBRIDGE, *in the State of* MASSACHUSETTS.

GENTLEMEN,

I THANK you for this addreſs, ſubſcribed by ſo large a number of reſpectable

 names,

names, and for the expreſſion of your ſatisfaction in my adminiſtration.

Difficulties were the inheritance to which I was born, and a double portion has been alotted to me. I have hitherto found in my integrity, an impenetrable ſhield, and I truſt it will continue to preſerve me.

I pity the towns which under the guidance of raſh or deſigning men, aſſembled without the neceſſary information, and paſſed reſolutions, which have expoſed them to cenſure.

I receive and return with pleaſure your congratulations on the preſent appearances of national union, and thank you for your aſſurances of ſupport.

JOHN ADAMS.

To JOHN ADAMS, PRESIDENT *of the* UNITED STATES *of* AMERICA.

SIR,

WE, the inhabitants of the town of Medford, in the State of Maſſachuſetts, approach you with reſpect and veneration; not ſolely becauſe you fill a high and important ſtation, —but becauſe you fill it with uprightneſs, dignity and honor.

When moſt of the governments of the old world are agitated to their centres, and by the

the insidious policy of the agents, those whom we have been accustomed to view as friends, our nation is menaced by a similar calamity :—When to moderate, and equitable demands for redress of wrongs, nothing has been received but a reiteration of insults and an accumulation of injuries ; the crisis seems to demand a public expression of attachment to the constitution and government of our country. We consider it an absurd and ridiculous assumption, that all the various descriptions of mankind should be capacitated to judge of the advantages or disadvantages of treaties—of the propriety of war, or of peace. Happily for the American people, those high attributes of national sovereignty are delegated to such a number, as is best to produce and secure the union of liberty with the good government of laws.

Should our confidence be misplaced, a strong and effectual remedy is provided in the revolution of elections. We therefore disclaim the doctrine of the right "to clog the wheels of government."—We would only declare, that the system which under the late and present administration, has been productive of so much national prosperity, as it commands our warmest attachment, so it is entitled to our most energetic support: —That, though the sentiments for peace universally pervades the nation, yet there is a point of degradation to which the just pride

of

of Americans will never ſuffer them to ſtoop; and, that ſooner than yield our liberties to anarchical deſpotiſm, an appeal to the laſt reaſon of ſtates, becomes the higheſt duty of freemen. In fine, we cordially obey the ſolemn dictates of the preſent eventful moment, to rally round the conſtitution and government of our country. and on the altar of freedom, once more ſwear to preſerve and defend them—once more pledge thereto—"our lives, our fortunes, and our ſacred honor."

To the INHABITANTS *of* MEDFORD, *in the State of* MASSACHUSETTS.

GENTLEMEN,

I THANK you for this addreſs—expreſſive as it is conciſe—which has been preſented to me by your repreſentative in Congreſs, Mr. Sewall.

The advantages and diſadvantages of treaties, and the propriety of war or peace, depend commonly upon a ſyſtem of information ſo complicated, that it requires all the time of the people to poſſeſs themſelves of it; and frequently much of it is of a nature which cannot be laid open to public view. It ſeems therefore inevitable, that thoſe high attributes of national ſovereignty, ſhould be delegated to ſuch a number as is

beſt

beſt calculated to produce and ſecure the union of liberty with the government of laws.

Your declaration, that the ſyſtem of the late and preſent adminiſtration commands your warmeſt attachment, and is entitled to your moſt energetic ſupport, becauſe it has been productive of ſo much national proſperity, is very conſolatory.

The oath you have again taken on the altar of freedom, to preſerve your conſtitution and government, will be regarded by all who know you as ſolemn and ſincere—not like thoſe of eternal enmity to tyranny and anarchy, taken by thoſe moderns, who by their arts and arms, are daily extending and propagating both.

There is indeed a point of degradation to which the juſt pride of Americans will never ſuffer them to ſtoop. Sooner than yield our liberties to anarchical deſpotiſm, an appeal to the laſt reaſon of republics, becomes the higheſt duty of freemen.

JOHN ADAMS.

To the PRESIDENT *of the* UNITED STATES.

SIR,

A NUMBER of the inhabitants of Dedham, and other towns in the vicinity, in the county of Norfolk, in Maſſachuſetts, aſſem-

 bled

bled at Dedham, to commemorate the 4th of July, '76; having been led by the occasion to consider the insults, perfidy, and hostile aggressions of France against the United States, presume to address you their sentiments on the present aspect of public affairs.

Many, too many, considered independence, when it was recognized by the peace of '83, as a condition of perpetual national repose. By repressing our own ambition, and pursuing a just and pacific policy, so obviously the wisest for the United States, and which we acknowledge its government has most faithfully pursued, they supposed one half the causes, that engender wars, would be removed; and, as a security against the contingency of the other half, they relied on the interest of foreign nations to court our friendship, as well as on the slenderness of their motives to provoke our hostility.

These hopes, and half the foundation for them, were fallacious; and most of all have they proved false in our blind dependence on the faith and justice, the friendship and gratitude of France.

From political misinformation, which, we regret to say, has been peculiarly active in the scene we inhabit, too many have believed, that France, though crushed under the iron rigor of a military despotism, enjoyed liberty;

liberty; that the inordinate thirst of her rulers for dominion, was inspired by a generous zeal to set oppressed nations free; that these nations were emancipated by being subdued; and, though they lost their independence, they were gainers by some unknown equivalent, gratuitously conferred by their conquerors. If, besides the absurdity of these opinions, you should discern in them something like infatuation and debasement, you will ascribe it, Sir, to its proper cause. The government of France and its emissaries, while they despised and outraged the ever venerable *principles* of liberty, practised amongst us a successful imposture with the *name*. But, by the publication of the diplomatic correspondence with France, the period of infatuation has, we trust, passed over—not indeed without some temporary discredit to the sobriety and steadiness of the American character; but we hope with much solid and lasting instruction to our nation. We think it candid, however, to declare our belief, and events have confirmed it, that many, in the midst of their delusion for France, preserved a superior affection for their own country. We have indeed generally thought too well of France, and France too meanly of us—too meanly of our spirit and union. But she will learn that we will bear no foreign yoke—we will pay no tribute. And we beg leave to assure you,

you, Sir, that we perceive the fruitleſſneſs, we might ſay the fatal raſhneſs, as well as meanneſs of truſting any further to delaying counſels, and deluſive negociations. We ſee alſo, and we lament, that our nation has ſeen ſo late, that the ſafe keeping of American independence is, like that of every other free ſtate, in the energy of its ſpirit and reſources; nor will we diſgrace ourſelves by heſitating a moment between war and ſubmiſſion to the exactions of France. Yet ſuch is the alternative plainly before us.

If our fathers had not felt ſentiments like theſe, they would not have gained independence, and if we did not feel them, it would not reach poſterity.

To the INHABITANTS *of* DEDHAM, *and other Towns in its vicinity, in the County of* NORFOLK, *in* MASSACHUSETTS.

GENTLEMEN,

I THANK you for a friendly addreſs, preſented to me by your repreſentative in Congreſs, Mr. Otis.

No faithful and intelligent American could paſs the 4th of July, this year, without ſtrong ſenſations and deep reflections, excited by the perfidy, inſolence, and hoſtilities of France. The ideas of never ending repoſe in America, were as viſionary as the projects

projects of universal and perpetual peace, which some ingenious and benevolent writers have amused themselves in composing.

We have too much intercourse with ambitious enterprizing and warlike nations; and our commerce is of too much importance in their conflicts, to leave us a hope of remaining always neutral. Although our government has exhausted all the resources of its policy in endeavours to avoid engaging in the present uproar, neither the faith, justice or gratitude of France would suffer it to succeed.

I know very well that political misinformation has been peculiarly active in the scene which you and I inhabit, and that too many have believed that France, though crushed under the iron hand of a military despotism, enjoyed liberty; that the inordinate ambition of her rulers for dominion was infused by a generous zeal to set oppressed nations free; that these nations were emancipated by being subdued, and though they lost their independence, they were gainers by some unknown equivalent gratuitously conferred by their conquerors.

If impostures so gross, have had too much success, America is of all the people of the world the most excuseable, for many particular reasons, for their credulity. The people of a great portion of Europe have been

more

more fatally deceived; even the people of England, with all their national antipathies, and under all the energies of their government, have been equally misinformed, and appear to be now more affected with remorse. The sobriety and steadiness of the American character, will not suffer more discredit than other nations, and we have certaily apologies to make peculiar to ourselves.

That all Americans by birth, except perhaps a very few abandoned characters, have always preserved a superior affection for their own country, I am very confident; that we have thought too well of France, and France too meanly of us, I have been an eye and ear witness for twenty years. These errors on both sides must be corrected—she will soon learn that we will bear no yoke, that we will pay no tribute.

For delaying counsels, the constitution has not made me responsible; but while I am entrusted with my present powers; and bound by my present obligations, you shall see no more delusive negociations. The safe keeping of American independence is in the energy of its spirit and resources. In my opinion, as well as yours, there is no alternative between war and submission to the Executive of France. If your fathers had not felt sentiments like these, they would have

have been "hewers of wood" to one foreign nation; and if you did not feel them, your posterity would be "drawers of water" to another.

JOHN ADAMS.

To JOHN ADAMS, PRESIDENT *of the* UNITED STATES.

SIR,

AS inhabitants of this ancient town which gave you birth, although now by its division, Quincy is honored as the place of your residence, we retain that affection and esteem for your personal honor and happiness, which are the natural result of such a connection; yet this is a circumstance of very small consideration, compared with other reasons of attachment and veneration, which upon this trying crisis of political emergency, we beg leave to offer in the following address.

Your promotion, Sir, by the merited suffrages of a free people, to the chief seat of government is a circumstance of pre-eminence and honor to which despotic and hereditary princes, can never attain. Being thus made by your country, the centre of their national dignity, confidence and affection, we glory in your great and acknowledged abilities as a statesman, and in your unabated

unabated zeal, unſhaken fortitude and perſerverance as a patriot; all which qualities have long ſince been rendered conſpicuous to your fellow citizens, and to the world, in your political and eminent ſervices.

We contemn, Sir, as we know you do, the fawning paraſite; the flattering ſycophant, as a reproach to merited honor; a vermin, that mars the tree moſt to which its attachments are apparently the greateſt. We ſhould not therefore preſume thus freely to expreſs the juſt ſenſibilities of our hearts, in language that would bear the remoteſt reſemblance to that praiſe, ſo often unjuſtly laviſhed upon tyrants, to anſwer ends as baſe as their encomiums are falſe, were it not to contradict the envenomed pens and tongues of reproach and ſlander, which with uncontrouled licence, have been attempting to tarniſh the character, with the honor, probity, and firmneſs of which are intimately connected the political glory, ſafety and happineſs of theſe united, ſovereign and independent States.

Were you the man, Sir, intriguing for Britiſh influence, and to yield up the independent glory of United America, to the nation from whoſe unconſtitutional exactions you had the honor of being eminently inſtrumental in procuring our deliverance; or were you ſecretly exerting your abilities

to

to prevent a compromiſe with France, for an amicable ſettlement of all real, or imaginary injuries of which they complain, as has been ſo often, ſo confidently, and we fear much worſe than ignorantly announced to the public, and which many, too many, have been betrayed to believe, we ſhould now with unſufferable regret, have to lament in our firſt magiſtrate, an inſtance of apoſtacy, unequalled in the page of civil hiſtory. You will then, Sir, pardon our enthuſiaſm, while in your letter of credence to the French Directory, and the liberal, pacific inſtructions to our envoys, we ſee the diſorganizing deſigns of the ſecret enemies of our unrivalled proſperity, as in a moment defeated; and in ſpite of malignity itſelf, the honor of our Executive and government at large eſtabliſhed by evidence that enforces conviction.

The joyous effects are every where viſible! At the return of harmony in Congreſs, the heart of every true friend to America exults; the people, who in great numbers before, alarmingly ſeparated in affection and confidence from their own government, and rendered jealous of the firſt characters of their own election, convinced of the ſnares ſpread for their country by foreign intrigue, are now crowding to its ſtandard, and conſecrating their fortunes and lives for its defence. So ſignal a providence for the

G detection

detection of fraud, and the coalition of a people divided and consequently sinking into inevitable destruction, is perhaps a novelty in the annals of nations.

While solemnly grateful to the all-discerning eye of Divine Benevolence, which has brought to light those hidden things of darkness, by which so many of us have been so unhappily deceived, we congratulate our country at large, that numerous private friendships which were violated, and otherwise good neighbours and important connexions, estranged from one another, are now returning with mutual extacy, to the fraternal embrace. The uninformed and unreasonably impassioned only stand at a forbidding distance.

Disgusted at the illiberal arts and avarice of those with whom our envoys are admitted to converse, and at the refusal of audience by the French Directory, after so friendly an advance, accompanied too with every mark of respectful attention to so great a people, a revolt from our over heated affection for such a government, cannot fail of being the consequence. Sincere and ardent were our attachments to the interests of the French nation, while they stood on their own defence, and preserved a spirit limited by the decisions of reason; but when universal empire seems to be adopted as their object,

object, and the darkneſs of intrigue as a favorite meaſure to accompliſh their nefarious deſigns; when the price of friendſhip with America is the proſtitution of her wealth, her honor, her independence—it muſt be our duty to reprobate her pride, and ſpurn her inſulting demands. Nor can the genuine ſons of America, although friendly to France, and with their illuſtrious Executive, deſirous of forming an alliance upon foundations mutually juſt and beneficial, forbear pledging themſelves for the defence of their invaluable rights againſt the unprovoked invaſion with which we are threatened.

Acquieſcing, Sir, moſt cordially in your public adminiſtration; wiſhing you the guidance of heaven in every duty of your important and moſt difficult ſtation; and that the pen of ſlander, however artfully aimed, may never penetrate to diſturb your inward peace and tranquillity, or diſcourage your exertions, ſtill ſo needful for the proſperity of your country, we beg leave to ſubſcribe ourſelves your confirmed friends, &c.

To the INHABITANTS *of the Town of* BRAINTREE, *in the State of* MASSACHUSETTS.

GENTLEMEN,

THIS kind addreſs, from the inhabitants of a diviſion of the ancient and venerable

able town of Braintree, which has always been my home, is very obliging to me.

The tongues and pens of ſlander, inſtruments with which our enemies expect to ſubdue our country, I flatter myſelf have never made impreſſions on you, my ancient townſmen, to whom I have been ſo familiarly known from my infancy A ſignal interpoſition of providence, has for once detected frauds and calumnies, which, from the inexecution of the laws, and the indifference of the people, were too long permitted to prevail.

I am happy to ſee that your minds are deeply impreſſed with the danger of the preſent ſituation of our country, and that your reſolutions, to aſſert and defend your rights, are as judicious and determined, as I have always known them to be upon former occaſions.

I wiſh you every proſperity and felicity, which you can wiſely wiſh for yourſelves.

JOHN ADAMS.

From the Town of QUINCY, *in the State of* MASSACHUSETTS, *to the* PRESIDENT *of the* UNITED STATES.

SIR,

WE the ſubſcribers, inhabitants of your native town, being many of us the contemporaries

raries of your youth, cannot help looking back with pleafure and gratitude on your early exertions in favor of our liberty and independence. When the unreafonable demands of that country from whence we derived our origin, made it neceffary for us by fair reafon and argument to defend our rights as freemen, your early publications, almoft from the time of your leaving the univerfity, caufed the enemies of our independency, at that time, to watch you with a malignant yet fearful eye; and prefaged to them the greatnefs of your future abilities. We are happy in having lived to fee the exertion of them fucceeded in negociations of the moft important and difficult nature, with refpect to gaining our national independence; and in promoting that excellent form of government, under which we have voluntarily agreed to live.

But now, Sir, we are called to meet a different ftate of things. A nation, with whom we had been taught to expect the moft friendly intercourfe, is making violent depredations on our property, and refufes to hear our complaints. Stung with fuch conduct from a nation we had been wont to love, and difgufted at their haughty treatment of our ambaffadors and our country, we feel the neceffity of union among ourfelves, and that our unanimity fhould be known: We therefore beg leave, Sir, in this public manner, to aſſure you, that we entirely approve of the prudent, juſt and pacific meaſures that have been employed by the ſupreme Executive, in behalf of the United States, for accommodating all differences between them and France; and that if nothing ſhort of giving up our liberty, ſovereignty and independence will ſatisfy their luſt of power, we will freely ſacrifice our fortunes and our lives in defence of our freedom.

To the INHABITANTS *of the Town of* QUINCY, *in the State of* MASSACHUSETTS.

GENTLEMEN,

NEXT to the approbation of a good conſcience, there is nothing perhaps which gives us more pleaſure than the praiſe of thoſe we love moſt, and who know us the moſt intimately.

I could not receive your addreſs—in which I read with pleaſure inexpreſſible, the names of clergy and laity, officers and ſoldiers, magiſtrates and citizens of every denomination; among whom were the moſt aged, whoſe countenances I had reſpected; my ſchool-fellows and the companions of my childhood, whom I had loved from the cradle;—without the livelieſt emotions of gratitude and affection.

With you, my kind neighbours, I have ever lived in habits of freedom, friendſhip and

and familiarity; we have always agreed very well in principles and opinions; and well knowing your love of your country and ardor in its defence, your explicit declaration upon this occasion, though unexpected, is no surprize to me. Accept of the best wishes of a sincere and faithful friend, for a continuance of harmony among you, and for the prosperity of all your interests.

JOHN ADAMS.

To the PRESIDENT, *and to the* CONGRESS *of the* UNITED STATES.

WE the subscribers, inhabitants of Brookline, partaking of that anxious concern for the public welfare, which at this crisis is felt by all good citizens, beg leave to express our highest approbation of those honest and unwearied endeavours, which, under every discouragement, have been used by the Executive, to preserve our national peace. But while we witness with pleasure, that every thing just and honorable, which a sincere desire of conciliation could suggest, is offered by the United States, we see with extreme indignation, that France will harken to nothing but enormous contributions of money; and these contributions we are expressly told, are not the price of peace, but merely

of

of negociation. A compliance with these terms so arbitrary and unjust in themselves, and so degrading to an independent people, we conceive would soon be followed by fresh insults and exactions, until by degrees we should be reduced to a state of unconditional subjection: That such is the design as well as tendency of these demands, cannot be doubted, since they are enforced by threats of our national destruction; and the fate of Venice, plundered, divided and sold, after it was declared free, is held up to terrify us into submission—the deplorable situation of some, and danger of the other European republics is also drawn in just but sable colours with the same design—republics whose governments are subverted, whose treasuries are drained, and their credit exhausted, whose cities are overawed and their fields ravaged by a ferocious soldiery, and whose people uniformly plundered, impoverished and oppressed, are not allowed even the melancholy privilege of complaining. Such is the wretched fate with which *we* are threatened with, unless we comply with the demands of the Directory—demands which though arbitrary and unreasonable in the highest degree, are yet but the preliminaries of negociation, and not the conditions of peace.

Instructed, but not terrified, by these awful scenes of the Revolutionary drama, we trust

truſt that the American people, having all one intereſt in the ſafety of their common country, will with us have but one ſentiment concerning its defence. We are ſenſible that domeſtic diviſions have facilitated the ruin of the republics of Europe, and *their* deſtroyers plainly tell us, that the ſame diviſions exiſt here, and will enable them to effect a ſimilar ruin in the United States :—But ſo far as depends upon us, we will diſappoint this expectation, by proving to France and to the world, that we are inſeparably united, and are determined to preſerve our liberty and laws ſacred and inviolate, againſt every enemy.

As ſincere lovers of our country therefore, and faithful ſupporters of thoſe authorities which are entruſted with its welfare, we declare that we fully confide in their talents, experience and patriotiſm, to provide for every exigency, and that we will at every hazard ſupport the meaſures which they ſhall ordain.

To JOHN ADAMS, PRESIDENT, *the* SENATE, *and* HOUSE *of* REPRESENTATIVES *of the* UNITED STATES *of* AMERICA.

AT a period which ſo ſeriouſly arreſts the attention of every American, and true friend to his country, as the preſent, the inhabitants of of Lynn, in the State of Maſſachuſetts, feeling it be their duty, and impreſſed with the juſt, wiſe and prudent adminiſtration of the Executive, and the rulers in general of the American republic, ardently embrace an opportunity to announce their determined reſolution to ſupport their conſtitution and government, with all they hold moſt ſacred and dear. Convinced as we are, that the Preſident has, by fair, unequivocal and full inſtructions, which he has given to our envoys, to adjuſt and amicably accommodate all exiſting difficulties between the United States and the French republic, done all, conſiſtent with the honor, dignity and freedom of his country, to preſerve peace and good underſtanding with that nation. Notwithſtanding our envoys are commiſſioned with full power to ſettle all animoſities with the French agents, upon the broadeſt baſis of equity, they are treated with neglect—refuſed an audience, leſt their reaſonings ſhould ſhow to the world the integrity of our government; and diſcloſe their iniquity.

Legiſlators, Guardians! The moſt nefarious deſigns have been plotted to ſubvert our government, ſubjugate the country and lay us under contribution; but thanks be to the Sovereign of the univerſe, that we do not experience the fate of Venice, nor groan under the oppreſſion of ſubdued nations. We are a free people, have a ſenſe of the

bleſſings

blessings which we enjoy under that liberty and independence, which we have wrested from the hand of one king, and will not supinely submit to any nation.

We wish not again to behold our fields crimsoned with human blood, and fervently pray God to avert the calamities of war: Nevertheless, should our magistrates, in whom we place entire confidence, find it expedient to take energetic measures to defend our liberties, we will readily co operate with them in every such measure:—Nor do we hesitate at this interesting crisis, to echo the declaration of our illustrious chief, that "we are not humiliated under a colonial sense of fear; we are not a divided people." Our arms are strong in defence of our rights, and we are determined to repel our foe.

To the INHABITANTS *of* LYNN, *in the State of* MASSACHUSETTS.

GENTLEMEN,

YOUR address to the President, Senate, and House of Representatives, adopted at a legal town-meeting, has been presented to me by your representative in Congress, Mr. Sewall.

When the inhabitants of one of our towns assembled in legal form, solemnly declare themselves impressed with the wise, just and

prudent

prudent administration of their rulers in general; and that they will support their constitution and government, with all they hold most sacred and dear, no man who knows them, will question their sincerity.

The conviction you avow that the President has done all, consistent with the honor, dignity and freedom of his country, to preserve peace and good understanding with the French, is a gratification to me which I receive with esteem.

As the treatment of our envoys is without a possibility of justification, excuse or apology, I leave it to your just resentment. Your acknowledgment of the blessings you enjoy, under your liberty, and independence, and determination never supinely to surrender them, prove you to deserve them.

JOHN ADAMS.

To the PRESIDENT *of the* UNITED STATES.

SIR,

WE the Congregational Ministers of your native State, met in annual convention, feel ourselves called upon as men, as American citizens, and as public professors and teachers of Christianity, to address you at this solemn and eventful crisis.

While the benevolent spirit of our religion and office prompts our fervent wishes and prayers

prayers for the universal extension of rational liberty, social order, and christian piety, we cannot but deeply lament, and firmly resist those atheistical, licentious and disorganizing principles, which have been avowed and zealously propagated by the philosophers and politicians of France; which have produced the greatest crimes and miseries in that unhappy country, and like a mortal pestilence, are diffusing their baneful influence even to distant nations. From these principles, combined with boundless avarice and ambition, have originated not only schemes of universal plunder and domination, but insidious attempts to divide the American people from their rulers, and involve them in a needless, unjust and ruinous war; arbitrary and cruel depredations on their unoffending commerce; contemptuous treatment of their repeated messengers and generous overtures of peace; rapacious demands and insulting threats in answer to the most fair and condescending proposals.

In this connexion, we offer to you, sir, our tribute of affectionate esteem and gratitude, and to Almighty God, our devout praise, for the wise, temperate and benevolent policy, which has marked your conduct towards the offending power, and which has given a new and splendid example of the beauty and dignity of the Christian spirit, contrasted with the base and profligate spirit of infidelity. We alſo bleſs God for your firm, patriotic and important ſervices to our country, from the dawn of its glorious revolution, and for the conſpicuous integrity and wiſdom which have been conſtantly diſplayed both by you, Sir, and your excellent and beloved predeceſſor.

As miniſters of the Prince of Peace, we feel it to be our duty both to inculcate and exemplify the pacific ſpirit which adorns his character and doctrine. We remember his command to forgive and love our moſt injurious enemies. But neither the law of Chriſtianity nor of reaſon requires us to proſtrate our national independence, freedom, property and honor at the feet of proud inſatiable oppreſſors; eſpecially of a government, which has renounced the goſpel and its ſacred inſtitutions, and has transferred to imaginary or heathen idols, the homage due to the Creator and Redeemer of the world. Such a proſtration would be treaſon againſt that Being who gave us our ineſtimable privileges civil and religious, as a ſacred depoſit to be defended and tranſmitted to poſterity. It would be criminal unfaithfulneſs and treachery to our country, our children, and the whole human race.

The fate of Venice, and other countries ſubdued by France, though held up to intimidate us to degrading ſubmiſſion, ſhall teach

teach us a far different leſſon; it ſhall inſtruct us to ſhun that inſidious embrace, which aims not only to reduce us to the condition of tributaries, but to ſtrip us of the goſpel, the Chriſtian Sabbath and every pious inſtitution. Theſe privileges we conſider as the chief glory of our country; the main pillars of its civil order, liberty and happineſs; as on the other hand we view its excellent political inſtitutions, as, under God, the guardians of our religious and eccleſiaſtical privileges. This intimate connexion between our civil and Chriſtian bleſſings, is alone ſufficient to juſtify the decided part which the clergy of America have uniformly taken in ſupporting the conſtituted authorities and political intereſts of their country. While we forgive the cenſure which our order has received from ſome perſons on this account, we will ſtill, by our prayers and examples, by our public and private diſcourſes, continue the ſame tenor of conduct which has incurred this malevolent or miſguided abuſe.

Amidſt the faſhionable ſcepticiſm and impiety of the age, it is matter of conſolation and gratitude that we have a Preſident, who, both in word and action, avows his reverence of the Chriſtian religion, his belief in a Redeemer and Sanctifier of the world, and his devout truſt in the providence of God.

May

May that Being whose important favor you recently led us to implore, graciously answer our united prayers in behalf of our common country. May he preserve your valuable life and health, your vigor, firmness and integrity of mind, and your consequent public usefulness; and at length transfer you, full of days and honor, to the possession of an eminent and everlasting reward.

To the CONVENTION *of* CONGREGATIONAL MINISTERS *in the State of* MASSACHUSETTS.

GENTLEMEN,

THIS respectful and affectionate address, from the convention of the clergy of Massachusetts, not less distinguished for science and learning, candor, moderation, liberality of sentiment and conduct, and for the most amiable urbanity of manners, than for unblemished morals and Christian piety, does me great honor, and must have the most beneficial effects upon the public mind, at this solemn and eventful crisis.

To do justice to its sentiments and language, I could only repeat it sentence by sentence, and word for word; I shall therefore confine myself to a mere return of my unfeigned thanks.

JOHN ADAMS.

From

From the GRAND LODGE *of* FREE *and* ACCEPTED MASONS *of the Commonwealth of* MASSACHUSETTS, *to the* PRESIDENT *of the* UNITED STATES.

SIR,

FLATTERY, and a diſcuſſion of political opinions, are inconſiſtent with the principles of this ancient fraternity; but while we are bound to cultivate benevolence, and extend the arm of charity to our brethren of every clime, we feel the ſtrongeſt obligations to ſupport the civil authority which protect us. And when the illiberal attacks of a foreign enthuſiaſt, aided by the unfounded prejudices of his followers, are tending to embarraſs the public mind with reſpect to the real views of our ſociety, we think it our duty to join in full concert with our fellow-citizens, in expreſſions of gratitude to the Supreme Architect of the Univerſe, for endowing you with that wiſdom, patriotic firmneſs and integrity, which has characterized your public conduct.

While the independence of our country, and the operation of juſt and equal laws, have contributed to enlarge the ſphere of ſocial happineſs, we rejoice that our Maſonic brethren, throughout the United States, have diſcovered by their conduct, a zeal to promote the public welfare, and that many of them have been conſpicuous for their talents and unwearied exertions. Among these, your venerable predeceſſor is the moſt illuſtrious example; and the memory of our beloved Warren, who from the chair of this Grand Lodge, has often urged the members, to the exerciſe of patriotiſm and philanthropy, and who ſealed his principles with his blood, ſhall ever animate us to a laudable imitation of his virtues.

Sincerely we deprecate the calamities of war, and have fervently wiſhed ſucceſs to every endeavor for the preſervation of peace: But, Sir, if we diſregard the bleſſings of liberty, we are unworthy to enjoy them. In vain have our ſtateſman laboured, in their public aſſemblies, and by their midnight taper; in vain have our mountains and vallies been ſtained with the blood of our heroes, if we want firmneſs to repel the aſſaults of every preſumptuous invader. And while as citizens of a free republic, we engage our utmoſt exertions in the cauſe of our country, and offer our ſervices to protect the fair inheritance of our anceſtors; as Maſons we will cultivate the precepts of our inſtitution, and alleviate the miſeries of all who by the fortune of war, or the ordinary occurrences of life, are the proper objects of our attention.

Long may you continue a patron of the uſeful arts, and an ornament of the preſent generation.

generation. May you finiſh your public labors with an approving conſcience, and be gathered to the ſepulchre of your co-patriots with the benediction of your countrymen ; and finally, may you be admitted to that celeſtial temple, where all national diſtinctions are loſt in undiſſembled friendſhip and univerſal piece.

To the GRAND LODGE *of* FREE *and* ACCEPTED MASONS *of* MASSACHUSETTS.

GENTLEMEN,

AS I never had the honor to be one of your ancient fraternity, I feel myſelf under the greater obligations to you for this reſpectful and affectionate addreſs. Many of my beſt friends have been Maſons, and two of them, my profeſſional patron, the learned Gridley, and my intimate friend, your immortal Warren, whoſe life and death, were leſſons and examples of patriotiſm and philanthropy, were Grand Maſters ; yet ſo it has happened, that, I never had the felicity to be initiated. Such examples as theſe, and a greater ſtill in my venerable predeceſſor, would have been ſufficient to induce me to hold the inſtitution and fraternity, in eſteem and honor, as favorable to the ſupport of civil authority, if I had not known their love of the fine arts, their delight in hoſpitality, and devotion to humanity.

Your

Your indulgent opinion of my conduct, and your benevolent wishes, for the fortunate termination of my public labors, have my sincere thanks.

The public engagement of your utmost exertions in the cause of your country, and the offer of your services to protect the fair inheritance of your ancestors, are proofs that you are not chargeable with those designs, the imputation of which, in other parts of the world, has embarassed the public mind, with respect to the real views of your society.

JOHN ADAMS.

From the BOSTON MARINE SOCIETY, *to the* PRESIDENT *of the* UNITED STATES.

SIR,

AT a time, when the existence of our independence is struck at; the sovereign rights of our country violated, by the refusal to receive our ambassadors, specially commissioned as the ministers of explanation and concord; and this haughty and hostile aspect, accompanied with the most indiscriminate spoliations on our commerce, grounded on the false, contemptuous opinion, that we are a mercenary, defenceless and divided people; it surely becomes the duty of every citizen, and incorporated bodies in particular,

lar, publickly to expreſs ſentiments, which may convince the world, as well as the French nation, that they indignantly feel, dare reſent, and hope to avenge the injured and inſulted character of our common country.

Although it is not for nations to command, they certainly may deſerve ſucceſs. The arms of our country have too recently with effect reſiſted the claims of the firſt maratime power the earth ever knew, for her ſons to now meanly crouch to the inſatiable cupidity and diſtant domination of an inſolent and inferior foe.

When friendſhip becomes inſult, or is permitted only on excluſive terms, dictated and impoſed by a corrupted, and corrupting government, it is time to ſhake off ſuch a debaſing yoke. Better at once to commence generous enemies, than maintain a deceptive and precarious connexion with ſuch inſidious friends.

Had the French people confined their efforts to the annihilation of their monarchy and all its collateral props, and to the erection of any other ſyſtem of rule, the buſineſs and its local conſequences ought to have been left to themſelves: But when we find this nation, after having completely attained the profeſſed object of their warfare, with ſavage hoſtility, in many inſtances, and in others,

others, artfully aiming at the utter ſubverſion of the political, religious and ſocial inſtitutions of all other governments, which time, experience, and even freedom, have ſanctioned, they become the enemies of all mankind, and ought to be oppoſed by every country that has any pretenſions to principle, ſpirit, or patriotiſm.

Theſe, Sir, are our ſentiments; and we truſt they actuate, and glow, in the breaſts, and if neceſſary, will nerve the arm, of the great maſs of the free and enlightened citizens that compoſe the American nation; and who muſt rejoice that their beloved Waſhington has been ſucceeded by a man who treads with equal ſtep the honeſt, plain and ſtrait road, ſo ſtrictly followed by that wiſe and able ſtateſman.

Extenſive as the commerce of the United States has become under a popular government, wiſely adminiſtered, and diſtant as our ſhores lie from the European continent, wooden walls, are confeſſedly, our beſt defence. You, Sir, appear early, and juſtly to have appreciated this ſyſtem of protection. Many of this ſociety have been engaged in maritime warfare; and when their country again calls, they truſt, that under your pilotage, they ſhall not be found wanting.

A life like yours, ſo long ſucceſsfully employed in public energy, and patriotic effect, has

has now become an important object of preservation. May Heaven preserve it with invigorated health; and a kind Providence enable you to augment your well founded claims to national gratitude, by a faithful, firm discharge of the numerous duties, and momentous services, committed to you by the constitution and councils of our country, and in which Europe, and the world, may eventually be so much interested.

To the BOSTON MARINE SOCIETY.

GENTLEMEN,

I THANK you for this respectful address.—The existence of the independence of any nation cannot be more grossly attacked, the sovereign rights of a country cannot be more offensively violated, than by a refusal to receive ambassadors sent as ministers of explanation and concord;—especially if such refusal is accompanied with public and notorious circumstances of deliberate indignity, insult and contempt. Indiscriminate despoliations on our commerce, grounded on the contemptuous opinion, that we are a divided, defenceless, and mercenary people, are not so egregious and agravated a provocation offered to the face of a whole nation as the former. I rejoice that you indignantly feel; that you dare resent; and that you

you hope to vindicate, the injured and insulted character of our common country. When friendship becomes insult, or is permitted only on terms, dictated and imposed, it becomes an intolerable yoke, and it is time to shake it off.—Better at once to become generous enemies, than maintain a delusive and precarious connexion with such insidious friends. Whatever pretexts the French people, or a French prince of the blood with his train, or a combination of families of the first quality, with officers of the army, had for their efforts, for the annihilation of the monarchy: we certainly, far from being under any obligation, had no right or excuse to interfere for their assistance. If, by the collateral props of the monarchy, you mean the nobility and the clergy, which has followed the annihilation of them: All their revenues have been seized and appropriated by another prop of the old monarchy, the army;—and the nation is become (as all other nations of Europe are becoming, if French principles and systems prevail) a congregation of soldiers and serfs. The French Revolution has ever been incomprehensible to me; the substance of all that I can understand of it, is, that one of the pillars of the ancient monarchy, that is the army, has fallen upon the other two, the nobility and the clergy, broken them both down; the building has fallen of course;

and

and this pillar is now the whole edifice. The military ſerpent has ſwallowed that of Aaron and all the reſt.

If the example ſhould be followed through Europe, when the officers of the armies begin to quarrel with one another—five hundred years more of Barons' wars may ſucceed. If the French, therefore, will become the enemies of all mankind, by forcing all nations to follow their example, in the ſubverſion of all the political, religious and ſocial inſtitutions, which time, experience, and freedom have ſanctioned, they ought to be oppoſed by every country that has any pretenſions to principle, ſpirit, or patriotiſm.

Floating batteries and wooden walls have been my favorite ſyſtem of warfare and defence for this country, for three and twenty years. I have had very little ſucceſs in making proſelytes. At the preſent moment, however, Americans in general, cultivators as well as merchants and mariners, begin to look to that ſource of ſecurity and protection; and your aſſiſtance will have great influence and effect, in extending the opinion in theory, and in introducing and eſtabliſhing the practice.

Your kind wiſhes for my life and health, demand my moſt reſpectful and affectionate gratitude; and the return of my ſincere prayers for the health and happineſs of the

Marine Society at Boston, as well as for the security and prosperity of the military and commercial marine of the United States, in which yours is included.

JOHN ADAMS.

From the STUDENTS *of* WILLIAMS' COLLEGE, *to His Excellency* JOHN ADAMS, PRESIDENT *of the* UNITED STATES.

SIR,

THOUGH members of an infant institution, and of little comparative weight in the political scale of the union, we feel for the interest of our country.

It becomes every youth in whose breast dwells the least principle of honor, to come forward calmly and boldly to defend his country.

When we behold France, a great and powerful nation, exerting all her energy to undermine the vast fabrics of religion and government; when we behold her inculcating the disbelief of a Deity, of future rewards and punishments; when we behold her discarding every moral principle, and dissolving every tie which connects men together in society, which sweetens life and renders it worth enjoying; when we behold her brutalizing man, that she may govern him;

as

as friends to humanity, as sharers in the happiness of our fellow men, as citizens of the world, our feelings are deeply affected.

We commiserate the sufferings of our European brethren; we weep over the awful calamities of anarchy and atheism.

But when we behold this aspiring nation, not contented with her vast European dominions, but endeavouring to stretch her colossean empire across the Atlantic, every passion is roused; and our souls are fired with indignation. We see that her object is universal domination, we see that nothing less than the universal degradation of man will satisfy these merciless destroyers. But be assured, Sir, should the situation of our country require it, we are ready to oppose her with all our youthful energy, and risk our lives in defence of our national rights.

Untaught in the school of adulation or the court of sycophants, we speak forth the pure sentiments of independence, we give you our warmest approbation. We behold with patriotic pride, the dignified conduct of our chief magistrate, at this alarming crisis: We are highly pleased with that candor, firmness and moderation which have uniformly characterized his administration. Though measures decisive and energetic meet with censure from the unprincipled, the disaffected and the factious, yet virtue must eternally triumph.

triumph. It is this alone which can ſtand the teſt of calumny; and you have this conſolation, that the diſapprobation of the wicked is ſolid praiſe.

At this eventful period, our eyes are fixed upon you, Sir, as our political father; and under the protection of a wiſe Providence, we rely on your wiſdom and patriotiſm, with the co-operation of our national council, to perpetuate our proſperity: and we ſolemnly engage, that while our government is thus purely and virtuouſly adminiſtered, we will give it our whole ſupport.

Theſe, Sir, are the unanimous ſentiments of the members of Williams' College, who, though convinced of the evils of war, yet deſpiſe the eaſe and affluence of peace, when put in competition with national freedom and ſovereignty.

Accept, Sir, our warmeſt ſolicitude for your perſonal welfare.

To the STUDENTS *of* WILLIAMS' COLLEGE, *State of* MASSACHUSETTS.

GENTLEMEN,

I HAVE not been leſs ſurprized than delighted with an addreſs from one hundred and thirty ſtudents of Williams' College, preſented to me by the Preſident *pro tempore* of the Senate, Mr. Sedgwick.

So

So large a number in so recent an institution, as it shews the flourishing circumstances of our country at present, affords a most pleasing prospect of young citizens in a course of education, for the future government, instruction and service of the country.

The composition of your address, shews a respectable sample of your literary talents, as the principles and sentiments it contains do honor to your heads and hearts. It is impossible for the unperverted mind of youth to see the world filled with violence, as it was before the flood, and every virtue and every principle trampled under foot, without feeling their souls fired with a generous indignation. Your readiness to oppose the torrent with all your youthful energy, and risk your lives in defence of your national rights, is greatly to your honor.

The testimony of your opinion in favor of the candor, firmness and moderation of my administration, is the more valuable, as you have not been educated in the school of adulation, and speak the pure sentiments of independence.

When your eyes are fixed upon me, as your political father, you at once excite the affections of my heart, and make me feel my own insufficiency for the arduous duties of that important character. With the co-operation of the national councils and the virtues of our citizens, I despair not of the continuance of our national prosperity—the talents and energies of the rising generation are a sure pledge of our safety, and the growing importance of America.

JOHN ADAMS.

From the STUDENTS *of* HARVARD UNIVERSITY, *to His Excellency* JOHN ADAMS, PRESIDENT *of the* UNITED STATES.

SIR,

WE flatter ourselves you will not be displeased at hearing that the walls of your native seminary are now inhabited by youth possessing sentiments congenial with your own. We do not pretend to great political sagacity; we wish only to convince mankind that we inherit the intrepid spirit of our ancestors, and disdain submission to the will of a rapacious, lawless and imperious nation. Though removed from active life, we have watched with anxiety the interest of our country: We have seen a nation in Europe, grasping at universal conquest, trampling on the laws of God and nations, systematizing rapine and plunder, destroying foreign governments by the strength of her arms, or the pestilence of her embraces, and scattering principles which subvert social order, raise the storms of domestic faction, and perpet-

uate

uate the horrors of revolution: We have ſeen this ſame nation violating our neutral rights, ſpurning our pacific propoſals, her piratical citizens ſweeping our ſhips from the ſeas, and venal preſſes under her controul, pouring out torrents of abuſe on men, who have grown grey in our ſervice: We have ſeen her miniſters in this country inſulting our government by a daring, unprecedented and contemptuous appeal to the people, and her agents at home offering conditions, which ſlaves, whoſe necks have grown to the yoke, would reject with indignation. We have ſeen this, Sir, and our youthful blood has boiled within us. When, in oppoſition to ſuch conduct, we contemplate the meaſures of our own government, we cannot but admire and venerate the unſullied integrity, the deciſive prudence, and dignified firmneſs, which have uniformly characterized your adminiſtration. Impreſſed with theſe ſentiments, we now ſolemnly offer the unwaſted ardor and unimpaired energies of our youth to the ſervice of our country. Our lives are our only property; and we were not the ſons of thoſe who ſealed our liberties with their blood, if we would not defend with theſe lives that ſoil, which now affords a peaceful grave to the mouldering bones of our foreſathers.

To the STUDENTS *of* HARVARD UNIVERSITY, *in* MASSACHUSETTS.

GENTLEMEN,

THE companions, ſtudies and amuſements of my youth, under the auſpices of our *alma mater*, whom I ſhall ever hold in the higheſt veneration and affection, came freſh to my remembrance on receiving your addreſs.

The maxims of life, and the elements of literature, which have ever been inculcated, in that ancient ſeat of education, could produce no other ſentiments, in a juncture like this, than ſuch as you have condenſed into a form ſo conciſe, with ſo much accuracy, perſpicuity and beauty.

Removed from the ſcenes of intemperate pleaſures, occupied with books, which impreſs the pureſt principles, and directed by governors, tutors and profeſſors, famous for ſcience, as well as eminent in wiſdom, the ſtudious youth of this country, in all our univerſities, could not fail to be animated, with the intrepid ſpirit of their anceſtors: Very few examples of degenerate characters, are ever ſeen iſſuing from any of thoſe ſeminaries. It is impoſſible, that young gentlemen of your habits, can look forward with pleaſure to a long career of life, in a degraded country, in ſociety with diſgraced aſſoci-

ates.

ates.—Your first care should be, to preserve the stage from reproach, and your companions in the drama, from dishonor.

But if it were possible to suppose you indifferent to shame, what security can you have, for the property you may acquire, or for the life of vegetation you must lead? What is to be the situation of the future divine, lawgiver, or physician? the merchant, or navigator? the cultivator, or proprietor?

Your youthful blood has boiled, and it ought to boil. You need not, however, be discouraged. If your cause should require defence in arms, your country will have armies and navies, in which you may secure your own honor, and advance the power, prosperity and glory of your contemporaries and posterity.

JOHN ADAMS.

DISTRICT OF MAINE.

To the PRESIDENT *of the* UNITED STATES.

SIR,

ALTHOUGH we are sensible that the best reward for your great and distinguished services, is the consciousness that they have been performed from pure and honorable motives, we hold it to be the duty of all

all citizens, at this important crisis of our public affairs, to offer you their most sincere and unequivocal assurances of attachment and support.

In the ready and cheerful discharge of this duty, the subscribers, citizens of the town of Portland, in the District of Maine, beg leave to assure you that they entertain, not only the highest veneration for your character and person, but have a firm persuasion, that all the measures of your administration, and more particularly those which concern our foreign relations, have been the result of eminent wisdom and unshaken patriotism.

As a part of the American people, educated to the love and enjoyment of liberty, and in the habits of veneration for republican virtues, we have no language to express our indignation at the late measures of the French republic, originating in the most infamous and corrupt stratagems to annihilate our national soereignty. While every principle of duty and interest prompts us to unite in the preservation and defence of our excellent constitution, and in the support of those by whom it has been faithfully administered, we cannot but express our deep regret that the citizens of France do not seem to possess virtue sufficient to merit the blessings of a free government.

However

However wicked and hostile may be their designs upon us, our confidence, under the favor of Heaven, is in the fortitude and unanimity of our countrymen, to repress their pernicious effects; at the same time, that a nation, under the rod of despotism, and whose councils are distracted and corrupted, ought not to be feared.

For your firm and dignified resistance against the aggressions of our European enemies, we render you our warmest gratitude, and beg leave to repeat our assurances, that such measures as shall be devised by you and the Congress of the United States, for the preservation of our national honor and rights, shall meet our most decided and zealous support.

To the PRESIDENT *and* CONGRESS *of the* UNITED STATES *of* AMERICA.

AT a time when the agents of a foreign nation boasts of their intriguing talents, and of having a party in this country devoted to their interest, with whose aid they pretend they can impose on the people of the United States, and by their deceptive arts prevent them from uniting in opposition to the unreasonable and unjust demands of France; and at a time when so many attemps have been made, to defame the administration of our

our own government—The inhabitants of the town of Wells, have thought it expedient to addreſs you—and accordingly at their meeting held on the ſeventeenth of May, unanimouſly directed a committee choſen from among them, reſpectfully to declare to you, and through you to the world, their firm and unſhaken attachment to their country, its conſtitution, its laws, and conſtituted authorities—to declare to you their entire approbation of the meaſures from time to time, adopted by the ſupreme Executive of the nation, in reſpect to our foreign relations, and in particular towards the French republic—To declare to you their juſt indignation againſt thoſe enemies of our country, whether foreign or domeſtic, who have been buſy in ſowing the ſeeds of diſcord, and propagating an opinion, that we are a people divided from our government, and oppoſed to its meaſures—And at the ſame time to aſſure you, that although they deprecate the calamities of a war, yet repoſing the higheſt confidence in your patriotiſm, wiſdom and firmneſs, they will moſt cheerfully afford every ſupport in their power, for carrying into complete effect all ſuch meaſures as you ſhall deem neceſſary in defence of the country, and for ſecuring that freedom and independence which are equally dear to the American people and their government.

To

To the PRESIDENT of the UNITED STATES.

SIR,

AT this important crisis of our national affairs, we the subscribers, inhabitants of the town of Arundell, in the District of Maine, have conceived it our duty respectfully to express to you, our firm attachment to our federal constitution and government—and to give you the most unequivocal assurance, of our perfect approbation of your administration since you have presided over the interests of our common country; especially in the measures adopted in relation to the French nation. And while we behold, with indignation the vile insidious attempts of those enemies of our peace and happiness, whether in America or France, calculated to divide the people of the United States from their government, by sowing the seeds of discord and sedition amongst us, thereby to accomplish the subjugation of our infant republic; we beg leave to assure you, that placing the fullest confidence in your wisdom, firmness and integrity, and in the patriotism of every department of our government, we will cheerfully afford every support in our power to effectuate such measures as you and they shall deem expedient to adopt for the defence and protection of our country, its freedom and independence.

RHODE-ISLAND.

To the PRESIDENT *of the* UNITED STATES.

SIR,

THE General Aſſembly of the State of Rhode-Iſland and Providence Plantations, beg leave to expreſs their cordial approbation of your wiſe and pacific meaſures, in the attempt to negociate with the republic of France. They obſerve, with ſingular ſatisfaction, that you appear to have been actuated by a ſincere deſire to do juſtice to that republic, if in any thing ſhe had been injured; to obtain juſtice for the multiplied injuries which her citizens had committed againſt us; and, above all, to preſerve peace. We indulged a hope, that your overtures for reconciliation, dictated by a ſpirit of impartiality, and a love of juſtice, would have been heard with candor, and treated with reſpect. It is therefore with regret and aſtoniſhment we learn, that theſe unequivocal proofs of friendſhip have been diſregarded; that our envoys have not been accredited, and that the moſt liberal advances to negociation have been rejected. You have purſued peace with a ſolicitude correſponding with the importance of the object; and if it cannot be preſerved, the failure ought not to be attributed to any

want

want of liberality or justice in the means you have employed. We are satisfied that you could not have gone further toward the attainment of this object, without committing the honor and dignity of our country.

In the present state of our national affairs, when a foreign power has lost sight of the immutable principles of justice, and of the solemn faith of treaties, and cherishes the unfounded opinion that the people and government of the United States are divided, we consider it our sacred duty to declare to you, and to the world, that the government of our country have merited and obtained our affectionate confidence.

On an occasion so interesting, we feel the most lively pleasure in giving you every assurance of our confidence in your wisdom and integrity, and of our respectful and personal attachment. Relying, under God, upon the unanimity, courage and virtue of our fellow-citizens, we declare our solemn determination to support the constitution and government of the United States.

From the Town of NEWPORT, *to the* PRESIDENT *of the* UNITED STATES.

SIR,

AT this alarming crisis, when a foreign power cherishes the unfounded and dangerous

ous opinion, that the people and the government of the United States are divided, and is thereby encouraged to entertain the most hostile projects against *both* ; we consider it our duty, to declare to you and the world, that our affections are wedded to our constitution and our government, that all the objects of your administration, and the means by which they have been pursued, particularly as they regard the republic of France, challenge our most cordial approbation and grateful applause.

Believing peace to be the true policy of our country, we rejoice to find, by your instructions to our envoys, that you have endeavoured, by every prudent and honorable expedient, to avert the calamities of war, and to preserve undiminished, the public harmony and prosperity ; and we are conscious that you could not have gone further, in the pursuit of this object, without violating the good faith, prostrating the honor, or surrendering the independence of the United States.

On an occasion so interesting, we beg leave to offer you the assurances of our respect ; solemnly pledging ourselves, that, by uniting closely with the government, reposing in it a liberal confidence, acquiescing cheerfully in whatever burdens the public exigencies may require, we will, with zeal, with

with perſeverance, and all the energy of a people determined to be free and independent, reſiſt foreign influence, and repel foreign aggreſſion.

To the INHABITANTS *of* NEWPORT.

GENTLEMEN,

I THANK you for this cordial addreſs. When you declare to the world, that your affections are wedded to your conſtitution and government; that all the objects of my adminiſtration and the means by which they have been purſued, particularly as they regard the republic of France, challenge your moſt cordial approbation and grateful applauſe; that I have endeavoured, by every prudent and honorable expedient, to avert the calamities of war, and preſerve undiminiſhed, the public harmony and proſperity, and that I could not have gone further in purſuit of theſe objects, without violating the faith, proſtrating the honor, or ſurrendering the independence of the United States; that by uniting cloſely with the government, repoſing in it a liberal confidence, acquieſcing cheerfully in whatever burthens the public exigences may require, you will, with zeal and perſeverance, and all the energy of a people determined to be free and independent, reſiſt foreign influence and repel foreign aggreſſion;

aggression;—you deserve well of your country, and command my most hearty thanks.

JOHN ADAMS.

To the PRESIDENT *of the* UNITED STATES.

SIR,

THE underwritten, inhabitants of the town of Providence, voluntarily assembled, in pursuance of public notice, beg leave to address you, with sentiments of personal and profound respect.

The late disclosure of the views and designs of France, in contrast with the pacific disposition of the United States, has excited the most disquieting apprehensions of hostilities from that republic, and the most unlimited confidence, in the wisdom, integrity and patriotism of the administration of our government.

In the progress of the negociation with that republic, whose legitimate origin we were the first to acknowledge—a republic, which at the dawn of its political day, seemed elevated to the most sublime height of virtue, and disclaimed in the first exercise of its power, all right to interfere in the internal concerns of other nations, we observe, with regret, a departure from the great principles of liberty and justice; and we observe this with

with the deeper regret, becauſe that country received its firſt leſſon of liberty from ours.

After the numberleſs and trying proofs, which the United States had given of their ſincere deſire to preſerve an impartial neutrality; their repeated applications for redreſs, might at leaſt have been anſwered with profeſſions of amity and a love of juſtice; inſtead of an avowed intention, ſtill further to impoveriſh us, and to purſue a ſtudied ſyſtem of univerſal domination.

While we lament that ſome of the inhabitants of this country, have too much attached themſelves to European politics, we believe this dangerous miſtake proceeded not from a treacherous defection from the cauſe of their country, but from the faſcination of the brilliant ſpectacle, of a nation victoriouſly contending for its liberties.

We rejoice that the ſcales have now fallen from their eyes. They muſt now ſee, what enlightened ſtateſmen have ſeen before, that the ſacred name of *liberty*, is prophaned to diſguiſe projects of ambition and conqueſt.

Your late communications, muſt cement the public councils, and increaſe the energy of government.

The inadmiſſable, and exorbitant exactions of France, will not only deprive them of every American advocate, but convince the world, that an adjuſtment of the differences

ences between the two countries, was impracticable on any other basis, than the prostration of America at the feet of France. The result in the mind of every American must be, a manly determination to vindicate the honor and interest of his country.

Should we be driven to the last appeal, we have an extensive country full of resources, and we trust in God, who has hitherto so signally favoured us, that he will again inspire us with that glowing zeal, and undismayed courage, which, in a period not remote, this people so successfully displayed; and in such an exigency, we shall derive additional confidence, from the firm moderation, the long tried integrity, the ripened wisdom, which induced an enlightened nation, to place you at the helm of government.

We cannot close without assuring you of our entire approbation of your conduct in relation to the foreign concerns of this country, of our prayers for your personal health and happiness, and of our readiness, with our lives and fortunes, to support the dignity and independence of the United States.

To the INHABITANTS *of* PROVIDENCE.

GENTLEMEN,

THE respectful address from the inhabitants of Providence, who have been my friends

friends and neighbours from my youth, was by no means necessary to convince me of their affectionate attachment.

Imagination can scarcely conceive a stronger contrast, than has lately been disclosed between the views of France and those of the United States. I will not distinguish between the views of the governments and those of the nations; if in France they are different, the nation, whose right it is, will soon shew they are so; if in America they are the same, this fact also will be shewn by the nation in a short time in a strong light. I cannot, however, see in this contrast a sufficient cause of disquieting apprehensions of hostilities from that republic: hostilities have already come thick upon us by surprize, from that quarter—If others are coming, we shall be better prepared to meet and repel them.

When we were the first to acknowledge the legitimate origin of the French republic, we discovered at least as much zeal, sincerity and honesty of heart, as we did of knowledge of the subject, or foresight of its consequences—the ill success of those proofs which the United States have given of their sincere desire to preserve an impartial neutrality, and of their repeated negociations for redress of wrongs, have demonstrated, that other means must be resorted to, in order to obtain it.

I agree entirely with you in acquitting in general, thoſe of our citizens, who have too much attached themſelves to European politics. of any treacherous defection from the cauſe of their country. The French Revolution, was a ſpectacle, ſo novel, and the cauſe was ſo complicated, that I have ever acknowledged myſelf incompetent to judge of it, as it concerned the happineſs of France, or operated on that of mankind ; my countrymen in general, were, I believe as ill qualified as myſelf to decide ; the French nation alone, had the right, and the capacity, and to them it ſhould have been reſigned ; we ſhould have ſuſpended our judgments, and been as neutral and impartial between the parties in France, as between the nations of Europe.

The honor of our nation is now univerſally ſeen to be at ſtake, and its independence in queſtion, and all America appears to declare, with one heart and one voice, a manly determination to vindicate both.

The legiſlature, by the late publication of inſtructions and diſpatches, have appealed to the world, and if the iron hand of power has not locked up the preſſes of Europe, in ſuch a manner that the facts cannot be communicated to mankind, the impartial ſenſe, and the voice of human nature, muſt be in our favor. If perſeverance in injuſtice ſhould

ſhould neceſſitate the laſt appeal, whatever cauſes we may have to humble ourſelves before the ſupreme tribunal, we have none, for any other ſentiment, than the pride of virtue, and honeſt indignation, againſt the late conduct of France towards us.

I thank you, gentlemen, for your perſonal civilities to me, and return your kind wiſhes for my happineſs.

Your noble declaration of your readineſs, with your lives and fortunes, to ſupport the dignity and independence of the United States, will receive the applauſe of your country, and of all who have the ſentiments and feelings of men.

JOHN ADAMS.

To the PRESIDENT *of the* UNITED STATES.

SIR,

THE State Society of Cincinnati of Rhode-Iſland and Providence Plantations, aſſembled to celebrate the birth-day of our national independence, beg leave reſpectfully to addreſs you on the preſent momentous criſis of our public affairs. We have viewed the progreſs of your adminiſtration with that ſolicitude and anxiety which become free citizens, who know how to appreciate the bleſſings of liberty. And it is with extreme

treme regret, that we have observed the attempts of certain profligate and designing men to weaken the bond of national union, and diminish the respect due to the laws, the constitution, and the magistracy. But we are relieved from our apprehensions, by a clear conviction, that the firm, patriotic and enlightened policy pursued by the chief magistrate of the United States, supported by a great and respectable majority of our fellow-citizens, will not only protect our country from national insult and degradation, but place her on that point of elevation to which she is entitled by her courage, her virtues and successful struggle in the cause of freedom. With a sincerity void of duplicity, we assure you of our entire approbation of all the measures you have pursued to preserve the peace of our country; and it is with indignation we have witnessed every attempt to obtain an end so desirable to humanity, and the repose of nations, treated with insolence and contempt by a foreign power, whose insidious professions induced us to expect tranquillity, while her conduct bade us arm to support our sovereignty and independence, or tamely submit to be governed by "diplomatic skill" and foreign influence.—We are determined to live and die *free*—and we are ready *once more* to rally round the standard of our country, headed by that illustrious chief, who, at a time that

proved

proved the patriot and hero, led us to victory and independence. Every sacrifice which the future circumstances of our country may require, under whatever leader, we shall consider as nothing, when put in competition with the rights of a free, sovereign and independent nation—and we hope and trust by the blessing of Heaven, and the wisdom of our Executive, aided by the councils of the United States, and the generous efforts of her sons, that we shall be able to repel all foreign aggression, and transmit unimpaired our fair inheritance to latest posterity.

To the SOCIETY *of the* CINCINNATI, *in the State of* RHODE-ISLAND *and* PROVIDENCE PLANTATIONS.

GENTLEMEN,

I THANK you for your respectful remembrance of me on the birth-day of our United States.—The clear conviction you acknowledge of the firm, patriotic and enlightened policy, pursued by the chief magistrate of the United States, after a review of the progress of his administration, will encourage his heart, and strengthen his hands. —Our country, supported by a great and respectable majority of its inhabitants, will not only be protected from a degrading submission to national insults, but be placed, I

 trust,

truſt, on that point of elevation, where by her courage and virtues ſhe is entitled to ſtand. The beſt "diplomatic ſkill" is *honeſty;* and whenever the nation we complain of, ſhall have recourſe to *that*, ſhe may depend upon an opportunity to boaſt of the ſucceſs of her addreſs—till then ſhe will employ her *fineſſe* in vain. On the day you reſolved to live and die *free*, and declared yourſelves ready to rally round the ſtandard of your country, headed by that illuſtrious chief, who, at a time that proved the patriot and hero, led you to victory—I was employed in the beſt of meaſures in my power to obtain a gratification of your wiſhes, which I am not without hopes may prove ſucceſsful.—In a country like ours, every ſacrifice ought to be conſidered as nothing, when put in competition with the rights of a free and ſovereign nation; and I truſt, that by the bleſſing of Heaven, and the valor of our citizens, under their ancient and glorious leader, you will be able to tranſmit your faireſt inheritance to poſterity.

JOHN ADAMS.

From the STUDENTS *of* RHODE-ISLAND COLLEGE, *to the* PRESIDENT *of the* UNITED STATES.

SIR,

YOUR late communication to Congreſs, from our envoys to the French republic, excites

excites in our breasts the liveliest solicitude for the welfare of our country. We regret that your efforts amicably to accommodate the difficulties, in which we are at present involved, have not been attended with that success, which a confidence in your administration induced us to expect. With indignation we learn the humiliating conditions demanded of us by France, and trust they will never be complied with, while a drop of the American blood remains unshed.

During our late glorious struggle for independence, this seat of literature bore a distinguished part in the common calamities of our country. Her mouldering walls even now evince the cause in which she suffered. Sufficiently have we, already, experienced the evils of war;—sufficiently strong are the inducements which lead us to desire peace; yet to us, nothing can be more humiliating than to sacrifice our liberties, to avert the former, or preserve the latter. Sooner will we confederate with the great mass of our citizens, in the public cause, rally around the standard of liberty, resolved to live free, or perish by one noble effort, in the cause of violated liberty.

At a period, when such principles are avowed as threaten destruction to liberty, religion, and the repose of all nations, when the American character is debased and degraded,

graded, by false and calumnious insinuations; we hope we shall not be considered as deviating from propriety, by expressing our unfeigned approbation of your public conduct, and our fixed determination never to survive our national independence.

Accept, Sir, the most ardent desires of the students of this seminary, for the prosperity of the United States, and their united prayers for your health and happiness.

To the STUDENTS *of* RHODE-ISLAND COLLEGE.

GENTLEMEN,

THIS address, following so soon after those demonstrations of confidence, respect and affection, which I received from you, my amiable young friends, at your university, the last year, has tenderly affected my sensibility.

The solicitude you manifest for the welfare of your country, well becomes you, who have long to live, and as I hope, and believe have illustrious parts to act, in the naval, military, civil and religious institutions of society.

While I share, in your regrets for the ill success of my efforts to accommodate difficulties, my heart sympathizes in your generous

ous indignation, at the unworthy returns we have received, and with you, I truſt, that no diſgraceful demands will ever be complied with.

America in general, and your part of it in particular, though ever averſe to war, have always been familiar with it, becauſe from the firſt plantation of the country, they never could avoid it, for any long courſe of years.

The fifteen years of peace, which have been enjoyed, ſince the year 1782, is the longeſt period of tranquillity, perhaps, which we have ever enjoyed. The longer the peace, the greater averſion of the citizens to war, as many republicans of Europe have fatally experienced; in this conſideration, you may perhaps find ſome conſolation, if war cannot be avoided without a ſacrifice of honor.

Your unfeigned approbation of my public conduct is as honorable to me, as your fixed determination, never to ſurvive your national independence is glorious to yourſelves.

In return for your kind wiſhes, I ſincerely pray that you and your univerſity, may flouriſh forever in the happy fruits of liberty, literature, ſcience, morals and religion.

JOHN ADAMS.

CONNECTICUT.

To the PRESIDENT *of the* UNITED STATES.

SIR,

THE Legiſlature of the State of Connecticut is not in the habit of interfering in the adminiſtration of the general government, nor of obtruding opinions or advice upon the councils of the Union. We have been accuſtomed to exhibit, as a fair and ſufficient proof of our affection for the national conſtitution, an uniform obedience to the laws, and an undeviating reſpect for the conſtituted authorities; but at a time when the American nation is deeply injured and inſulted, by the lawleſs aggreſſions and imperious claims of a foreign power—when our enemies profeſs to confide in our diſunion, and boaſt of "the means" of ſevering the affections of our citizens from the government of their choice—it would ill comport with our duty or our feelings to repreſs the ſentiments with which we are animated.

That the United States, extenſively concerned in commercial intercourſe, ſhould be, in ſome degree affected by a war which deſolates Europe, was to be expected—But that a neutrality, ſtrict and impartial, ſhould be openly and inſidiouſly attacked—that intrigues, of a complexion and character the most formidable to our internal peace, should be industriously practised---that one ambassador should be refused an audience; and that three envoys sent expressly as the messengers of peace, should be treated with contemptuous neglect---or, for their overtures so just and honorable, demands the most insolent and insufferable should be substituted by the government of a nation assuming the high appellation of "a great and magnanimous republic," was not to be believed till realized, and can be ascribed only to a lust of domination which knows no bounds, and to an abandonment of the principles of morality and justice, without example in the history of the world.

Filled with astonishment and indignation, at events which threaten our national existence, we highly applaud the dignity and firmness, so conspicuously displayed by the Executive, and the prompt and efficacious measures adopted by the government, and we assure them of our firm and hearty support.

We deprecate war---but we cherish our independence;---it was won by a struggle too severe, to be easily surrendered. We revere the names, the virtues and the sufferings of our ancestors---The inestimable gift of civil and religious freedom derived from them, shall not be impaired on our hands; and no sacrifice of blood or treasure shall be esteemed

CONNECTICUT.

To the PRESIDENT *of the* UNITED STATES.

SIR,

THE Legiſlature of the State of Connecticut is not in the habit of interfering in the adminiſtration of the general government, nor of obtruding opinions or advice upon the councils of the Union. We have been accuſtomed to exhibit, as a fair and ſufficient proof of our affection for the national conſtitution, an uniform obedience to the laws, and an undeviating reſpect for the conſtituted authorities; but at a time when the American nation is deeply injured and inſulted, by the lawleſs aggreſſions and imperious claims of a foreign power—when our enemies profeſs to confide in our diſunion, and boaſt of "the means" of ſevering the affections of our citizens from the government of their choice—it would ill comport with our duty or our feelings to repreſs the ſentiments with which we are animated.

That the United States, extenſively concerned in commercial intercourſe, ſhould be, in ſome degree affected by a war which deſolates Europe, was to be expected—But that a neutrality, ſtrict and impartial, ſhould be openly and inſidiouſly attacked—that intrigues, of a complexion and character the moſt formidable to our internal peace, ſhould be induſtriouſly practiſed---that one ambaſſador ſhould be refuſed an audience; and that three envoys ſent expreſsly as the meſſengers of peace, ſhould be treated with contemptuous neglect---or, for their overtures ſo juſt and honorable, demands the moſt inſolent and inſufferable ſhould be ſubſtituted by the government of a nation aſſuming the high appellation of "a great and magnanimous republic," was not to be believed till realized, and can be aſcribed only to a luſt of domination which knows no bounds, and to an abandonment of the principles of morality and juſtice, without example in the hiſtory of the world.

Filled with aſtoniſhment and indignation, at events which threaten our national exiſtence, we highly applaud the dignity and firmneſs, ſo conſpicuouſly diſplayed by the Executive, and the prompt and efficacious meaſures adopted by the government, and we aſſure them of our firm and hearty ſupport.

We deprecate war---but we cheriſh our independence;---it was won by a ſtruggle too ſevere, to be eaſily ſurrendered. We revere the names, the virtues and the ſufferings of our anceſtors---The ineſtimable gift of civil and religious freedom derived from them, ſhall not be impaired on our hands; and no ſacrifice of blood or treaſure ſhall be eſteemed

od, we hope that an addreſs from the inhabitants of Hartford may be neither improper nor unacceptable.

Though we ſtrongly feel the indignities, which the United States have received from the temporary rulers of France, and lament their unprovoked depredations upon our commerce, yet ſince it is evident, that their momentary friendſhip could be purchaſed only by the ſacrifice of our wealth and independence; permit us to conſider the iſſue of your late endeavors to negociate with that haughty power, as a ſubject rather of juſt congratulation, than deſpondence.

The deſigns of foreign hoſtility, and the views of domeſtic treachery, are now fully diſcloſed. The moderation, wiſdom and dignity of our adminiſtration, have awed into ſilence the clamors of faction, and palſied the thouſand tongues of calumny. The ſpirit of the independent freemen is again awakened, and its combined force will be irreſiſtible. Situated at a happy diſtance from the deſperate contentions of oppreſſive monarchies, and unformed republics, while we continue firm and united, we can only be involved in the ſkirts of that ſtorm, which ſhakes Europe to its foundations. Internal faction and treaſon alone can endanger our government; and we are happy to find that theſe exiſt only in the feeble efforts of a few diſappointed

disappointed partizans. Though some of the southern states have been artfully misrepresented, as opposed to the federal government, and enemies to its administration, we do not hesitate to express our confidence in the collected firmness and wisdom which they have ever displayed on the approach of real danger. Nor can we doubt that they will join us with equal spirit to crush every attempt at disorganization, disunion and anarchy. The malignant leaders of faction, who for their own advancement, would overspread America with discord and slaughter, or destroy us in the insidious embraces of foreign fraternization, must prepare to meet the indignation of the people, whom they so long attempted to deceive, and to feel their influence annihilated on the discovery of their efforts and designs.

Relying, with perfect confidence, on the wisdom and patriotism of your administration, on the increasing firmness of the legislature, and the strength and union of the people, we humbly trust that the hand of Providence, which has supported us through greater perils, will enable us to withstand the arts or attacks of the foreign or internal enemies of our freedom.

In us you will ever find, not the servile partizans of Britain, France, or any external domination, but men glorying in the rights of American independence, and warm-

ly

NEW-YORK.

From the CITIZENS *of* NEW-YORK, *to the* PRESIDENT, SENATE, *and* HOUSE *of* REPRESENTATIVES *of the* UNITED STATES.

A NUMBER of reſpectable citizens of this place, aſſembled together, conſidering our preſent ſituation, with reſpect to the republic of France, as forming an important criſis in our public affairs; and feeling the warmeſt attachment to the conſtitution, and an unſhaken confidence in the conſtituted authorities of our country, conceived that at this time, to evidence that attachment, and that confidence, could not but be uſeful to our common intereſts, and acceptable to thoſe who direct our public councils.

They therefore appointed a committee to convey to the Executive of the United States, and to both Houſes of Congreſs, their approbation of the meaſures purſued by the Executive, in the late negociation with France; to aſſure them of their unabated confidence of our rulers; and of their readineſs and zeal to forward and ſupport every meaſure which ſhall be directed for the intereſt, and the honor of our country.

In communicating theſe ſentiments, our minds were naturally led to a review of the conduct

conduct of our government towards the French republic; and in that review, it is with pleasure we observe that we have beheld it on every occasion, performing with the most perfect integrity and good faith, all its engagements to that country and evincing its regard by every act of friendship in its power, consistent with those duties which it owed to other nations.

While on the other hand, the conduct of France to this country has been a series of insult, depredation and menace, more becoming conquerors and masters than the friends and allies of a free and independent people.

Under different pretences, as variable as they have been futile, she has insulted our government, in the person of our chief magistrate; she has attempted to sow dissensions among our citizens, and to separate them from their government; she has in contravention of the faith of treaties, no less than of the laws of nations, despoiled our countrymen when engaged in a lawful commerce; and she has imprisoned their persons. To our mild remonstrances and our pacific overtures, for accommodation of differences and restoration of former friendship, she has answered only by fresh indignities. Not content with humbling our country by the refusal to receive an ordinary ambassador, sent to explain and conciliate, she has dis-

dained

NEW-YORK.

From the Citizens *of* New-York, *to the* President, Senate, *and* House *of* Representatives *of the* United States.

A NUMBER of respectable citizens of this place, assembled together, considering our present situation, with respect to the republic of France, as forming an important crisis in our public affairs; and feeling the warmest attachment to the constitution, and an unshaken confidence in the constituted authorities of our country, conceived that at this time, to evidence that attachment, and that confidence, could not but be useful to our common interests, and acceptable to those who direct our public councils.

They therefore appointed a committee to convey to the Executive of the United States, and to both Houses of Congress, their approbation of the measures pursued by the Executive, in the late negociation with France; to assure them of their unabated confidence of our rulers; and of their readiness and zeal to forward and support every measure which shall be directed for the interest, and the honor of our country.

In communicating these sentiments, our minds were naturally led to a review of the

conduct

conduct of our government towards the French republic; and in that review, it is with pleasure we observe that we have beheld it on every occasion, performing with the most perfect integrity and good faith, all its engagements to that country and evincing its regard by every act of friendship in its power, consistent with those duties which it owed to other nations.

While on the other hand, the conduct of France to this country has been a series of insult, depredation and menace, more becoming conquerors and masters than the friends and allies of a free and independent people.

Under different pretences, as variable as they have been futile, she has insulted our government, in the person of our chief magistrate; she has attempted to sow dissensions among our citizens, and to separate them from their government; she has, in contravention of the faith of treaties, no less than of the laws, of nations, despoiled our countrymen when engaged in a lawful commerce; and she has imprisoned their persons. To our mild remonstrances and our pacific overtures, for accommodation of differences and restoration of former friendship, she has answered only by fresh indignities. Not content with humbling our country by the refusal to receive an ordinary ambassador, sent to explain and conciliate, she has disdained

dained even to treat, in the usual forms, with the extraordinary ministers, who in the persevering spirit of peace and accommodation were afterwards deputed; as if anxious to accumulate disgrace upon us, she held out to them the most humiliating terms; they were told that merely to entitle them to a hearing, their country must become tributary; and they were impliedly menaced that the American republic would be erased from the list of nations, if the resentment of France was not appeased!!!

Of such conduct there can be but one opinion. To such terms, freemen can give but one reply. To you, fathers of our country, it belongs to give that reply; and we are persuaded it will be such as becomes Americans.

For ourselves and those whom we represent, to our virtuous and independent chief magistrate, we say; that while the wisdom and moderation in which he has conducted the late negociation with France, have raised him in our esteem, his patriotism and unshaken firmness have rivetted him in our confidence.

To our fellow-citizens in the Senate and House of Representatives, we, declare, that conscious of the rectitude of our country's conduct, and deeply impressed with a sense of the wrongs she has sustained, we are determined

termined to support at all hazards, such measures as shall be deemed necessary to maintain her honor, her freedom and her independence.

To the CITIZENS *of* NEW-YORK.

GENTLEMEN,

YOUR address to the President, Senate and House of Representatives of the United States, has been transmitted to me, by your committee.

Among all the resolutions that have been taken, and addresses which have been presented at this important crisis, I know of none which have expressed sentiments more just, approbation and confidence more entire, or resolutions more patriotic and decided, and consequently none which will give more satisfaction to the public and to the legislature, or which has more cordially and deservedly, my thanks.

JOHN ADAMS.

To the PRESIDENT *of the* UNITED STATES.

SIR,

AT a time when you are receiving from every part of the Union, testimonies of respect for your character, and approbation

 of

of your measures, permit the Young Men of the city of New-York, to join the general voice of their countrymen, and express to you the gra itude, esteem and confidence with which your conduct has inspired them.

We have not the vanity to suppose, that the applause of inexperienced youth, can afford any high gratification to your mind, conscious as it must be of its own integrity and resources. In seasons of peace and tranquillity, we should have been restrained by that diffidence becoming our years, from mingling in affairs which have been committed to abler hands.—But in the hour of danger, when our shores are threatened with ravage by the republic of France, and our constituted authorities with dissolution; when our political rulers are treated with indignity, and we with our fellow-citizens charged with disunion and disaffection to our government, a sense of truth and the feelings which our wrongs have excited, induce us thus publicly to declare our unshaken attachment to our country, and our determined resolution to support those measures which its administration may direct or advise for its security.

We once were attached to France; it was an enthusiasm in favor of liberty. If that enthusiasm has ever drawn from us, in common with some of our countrymen, demonstrations

ſtrations of attachment upon which its rulers have founded their belief, that we are unfriendly to our government, we conſider it as a cauſe of regret, but we aſſure you, that the ſame enthuſiaſm now unites us more cloſely in the defence of our country, and inſpires us with a ſpirit of reſiſtance againſt the efforts of that republic to deſtroy our independence. Holland and Venice are inſtructive leſſons to the United States, of the inſecurity of too much forbearance, and the danger of miſplaced confidence; but, we need not appeal to the example of other nations. The multiplied and unprovoked aggreſſions of France, and her injurious and inſulting treatment to our miniſters of peace, are ſufficient to arouſe all the energies of the ſoul, and to intereſt every feeling of the heart in the cauſe of our country. Regardleſs of the faith of treaties, and in violation of the laws of nations, her rulers authoriſe the capture of our veſſels and the impriſonment of our citizens, attempt to ſow diſſenſion among our countrymen, and to fill the meaſure of their injuſtice, they ſpurn the olive branch offered by our government, and refuſe to liſten to us, unleſs upon terms to which freemen diſdain to ſubmit; thus injured, inſulted and threatened, reſentment becomes a virtue, and reſiſtance a duty which we owe to ourſelves and to poſterity; to us our liberty and independence, our country

country and religion, are dearer than life; when our political rulers declare them to be in danger, every citizen who possesses the sentiments of a patriot or the feelings of a man, must unite, and by timely and spirited exertions protect them from sacrifice. We claim it as our right, as we know it to be our duty to be placed foremost in their defence, and if war only can preserve them, we are prepared to meet it with becoming resolution.

Confident in such a cause of the support of our parents and friends, the consolations of conscience and the approbation of God, we pledge ourselves to you and to the world, that if our country should be assailed by foreign invasion or domestic treason, we will fly to its assistance at a moment's warning, and at the hazard of our lives, protect its government and independence.

To the YOUNG MEN *of the City of* NEW-YORK.

GENTLEMEN,

I RECEIVED this becoming, amiable and judicious address, from the Young Men of the city of New-York, with great pleasure.

The situation in which nature has placed your State, its numerous advantages, and its population

population so rapidly increasing, render it of great importance to the Union of the nation, that its youth should be possessed of good principles and faithful dispositions. The specimen you have given in this address, could not be more satisfactory.

I assure you, my young friends, that the satisfaction with my conduct, which has been expressed by the rising generation, has been one of the highest gratifications I ever received; because if I have not been deceived in my own motives, I can sincerely say, that their happiness and that of their posterity, more than my own, or that of my contemporaries, has been the object of the studies and labors of my life.

Your attachment to France, was in common with Americans in general—the enthusiasm for liberty which contributed to excite it, was in sympathy with great part of the people of Europe. The causes which produced that great event were so extensive through the European world, and so long established, that it must appear a vast scheme of Providence, progressing to its end, incomprehensible to the views, designs, hopes and fears of individuals, or nations, kings or princes, philosophers or statesmen. It would be weak to ascribe the glory of it, or impute the blame to any individual or any nation; it would be equally absurd for any individ-

ual

ual or nation to pretend to wiſdom or power, equal to the mighty taſk of arreſting its progreſs or diverting its courſe. May the human race in general, and the French nation in particular, derive ultimately from it an amelioration of their condition, in the extenſion of liberty, civil and religious, in increaſed virtue, wiſdom and humanity. For myſelf, however, I confeſs, I ſee not how, nor when, nor where. In the mean time, theſe incomprehenſible ſpeculations ought not to influence our conduct in any degree. It is our duty to judge by the ſtandard of truth, integrity and conſcience, of what is right and wrong, to contend for our own rights, and to fight for our own altars and fireſides, as much as at any former period of our lives. In your own beautiful and pathetic language, the ſame enthuſiaſm ought now to unite us more cloſely, in the defence of our country, and inſpire us with a ſpirit of reſiſtance againſt the efforts of that republic to deſtroy our independence. If my enthuſiaſm is not more extravagant than yours has ever been, our independence will be one eſſential inſtrument for reclaiming the fermented world, and bringing good out of the maſs of evil.

The reſpect you acknowledge to your parents, is one of the beſt of ſymptoms. The ties of father, ſon and brother, the ſacred bands of marriage, without which thoſe connexions

nexions would be no longer dear and venerable, call on you and all our youth to beware of contaminating your country with the foul abominations of the French revolution.

JOHN ADAMS.

To JOHN ADAMS, President of the United States.

SIR,

WE, the citizens of Albany, having a lively ſenſe of the danger with which our country is threatened by a foreign nation, beg leave to communicate to you our entire approbation of your conduct at this critical period, and to aſſure you of our ſincere diſpoſition to ſupport, with zeal and firmneſs, whatever meaſures the government of the United States deem neceſſary to vindicate and maintain our national honor and independence.

The moderation which this country has uniformly manifeſted towards the French republic, notwithſtanding its repeated and unprovoked aggreſſions on our neutral and ſovereign rights, is an inconteſtible proof of our ardent ſolicitude to cultivate peace. But there is a point beyond which even the bleſſings of peace cannot be ſought without ſervility—That point has been recently fixed between France and America, by the inſo-

lent

lent demands made upon us; demands which we cannot submit to, without prostrating our independence, and sacrificing our best interests.

The presumptuous hope, announced by the agents of the republic to our envoys extraordinary, that the American people are divided from their government, indicates that a perfidious attachment to the cause of France, lurks among us. The fallacy of this hope, it is equally our duty and our interest to expose. We therefore solemnly pledge ourselves, in the most unequivocal manner, to sustain, with energy, the constituted authorities of our country, against all the machinations of its enemies, whether foreign or domestic.

Accept, Sir, of our best wishes that a gracious Providence may long preserve your precious life, and continue to direct your administration, and that when the measure of your days shall be filled, you may receive the glorious reward that is due to eminent virtue and patriotism.

To the CITIZENS *of* ALBANY, *in the State of* NEW-YORK.

GENTLEMEN,

THE address of the citizens of Albany, has been presented to me by their representative in Congress, Mr. Glen.

I could

I could not look over the long roll of reſpectable ſubſcribers, without the ſentiments of gratitude, eſteem and reſpect.

The lively ſenſe of the danger, you expreſs, with which our country is threatened by a foreign nation, is as well founded, as your approbation of my conduct at this critical period, and your ſincere diſpoſition to ſupport, with zeal and firmneſs, whatever meaſures the government of the United States ſhall deem neceſſary, to vindicate and maintain our national honor and independence, are agreeable to me, and ſatisfactory to the public.

The moderation of this country towards the French republic, is almoſt without example; it would not, certainly, have been ſo long continued, towards any other nation in the world—it is not only a proof of our deſire of peace, but of our particular attachment to France.

There is indeed a point, beyond which, a love of peace, and friendſhip to France, cannot be indulged without ſervility.

Although the French government appears to have adopted againſt us the moſt perfect ſyſtem of hoſtility in their power, it is not for me to ſay how long we ſhall ſhackle ourſelves, by reſerves of friendſhip to them.

That a perfidious attachment to France, lurks among us, is moſt certain. We may,

 however,

however, confole ourfelves at this time, that it contaminates very few native Americans, and I fhould hope not many naturalized ftrangers. Pledges like yours, will foon reduce the number of both.

Your kind wifhes, that a gracious Providence may preferve my life, and direct my adminiftration, are too affecting to be anfwered by me, but by prayers for the citizens of Albany and their pofterity forever.

JOHN ADAMS.

To the PRESIDENT *of the* UNITED STATES.

SIR,

WE, the citizens of Hudfon and its vicinity, in the county of Columbia, and State of New-York, confidering the prefent ftate and afpect of public affairs, and feeling in common with our fellow-citizens the wounds inflicted upon our country by the wanton and multiplied aggreffions of the French republic, which, fpurning all overtures for conciliation, has treated with marked indifference and contempt repeated meffengers of peace—added infult to injury, and is daily extending her acts of violence and outrage—her agents infolently boafting of the power and effect of her diplomatic fkill—of the party it has created within the United

States—

States—exciting oppofition and dividing the people from their government; while on ordinary and lefs alarming occafions, we confider this mode of manifefting our opinions to our conftituted authorities fuperfluous, if not improper, we cannot at this interefting moment remain filent.

Refpect to the opinion of mankind, juftice to ourfelves and fellow-citizens, and truth itfelf impel us to declare that we are not divided from the government of our choice—that we pride ourfelves in cherifhing and fupporting it as the fabric of our own hands, peculiarly made for ourfelves, adapted to our fituation, deliberately put together by the united wifdom and experience of men, who, unawed by defpotic power, always knew what it was to be free—That we are determined to preferve it entire, and to tranfmit it to pofterity untarnifhed and unimpaired; that whilft we perfectly accord with the meafures adopted and purfued by the Executive of the United States to effect conciliation and preferve peace with the French republic, we feel perfuaded that nothing confiftent with the national honor and intereft of our country has been omitted to accomplifh the defired object. As much therefore as we deprecate the evils of war, and value the bleffings of peace, we cannot hefitate a moment to forget thofe evils when impelled by duty and neceffity, to affert and preferve preſerve our ſovereign rights and independence. With entire confidence in the long tried wiſdom, firmneſs and patriotiſm of the Preſident of the United States, and in the councils of the nation, we feel cheerfully diſpoſed with ſpirit and fortitude to meet any event which the preſent ſtate of things may produce, or the deſtiny of our country incur.

To the CITIZENS *of* HUDSON *and its vicinity, in the County of* COLUMBIA, *and State of* NEW-YORK.

GENTLEMEN,

YOUR declaration has been preſented to me by your Repreſentative in Congreſs.

The preſent aſpect of public affairs is indeed portentous, and the wounds inflicted on our country, by the wanton and multiplied aggreſſions of the French republic, muſt be felt by every American citizen who is faithful and true—Inſult has been added to injury until the meaſure is full.

The reign of terror and ſeduction, which began at Paris, has been extended in Europe as far as the Grand Monarch extended it, and is now attempted on this ſide the Atlantic; but we ſhould remember that Italy and the Netherlands have often been conquered by France, and that ſhe has as often been driven from her conqueſts with ignominy.

Your

Your attachment to the conſtitution, approbation of the adminiſtration, and confidence in the councils of the nation, are very ſatisfactory.

JOHN ADAMS.

To JOHN ADAMS, PRESIDENT *of the* UNITED STATES.

SIR,

WE, the Grand Jurors for the body of the county of Columbia, in the State of New-York, beg leave to addreſs you upon the preſent eventful period in our national affairs.

The late communications made by you to the legiſlature of the union, exhibit a criſis in our relations to the French republic, which, as it menaces our independence, awakens our zeal, and draws cloſer our affections to the government by which alone our independence can be ſecured. We ſee, with indignation, the inſinuations of a foreign power, that there are citizens of the United States ſo regardleſs of that diſtinguiſhing and impreſſive title, and ſo loſt to a ſenſe of duty, as to be capable of being made the diſgraceful inſtruments of counteracting the meaſures of their own free government, and of proſtrating it at the feet of foreign domination; and though we truſt that every hope derived from this ſource will prove deluſive, yet we are conſtrained to ſeparate ourſelves from thoſe unworthy individuals and abandoned parricides, if any ſuch there be, who may have encouraged it. If the good wiſhes heretofore expreſſed by our citizens for the liberty and proſperity of France, ſincere and ardent as they were, ſhould have led to the ſuppoſition that their affections might be alienated from their own free, legitimate government; or that they would abet or ſanction ſchemes of aggrandizement in one nation at the expenſe of the ſovereignty of others, we feel a full confidence that the idea will be repelled with indignation, and that it will be evinced that an adherence to *principles* conſtitutes *American character*, and that in our attachment to liberty, we know how to diſtinguiſh between the ſemblance and the reality, the empty profeſſion and the ſolid enjoyment of that bleſſing. In contemplating our government as a free repreſentative republic, we recognize in its very ſtructure ſolid grounds of liberal confidence, and it is with equal pride and pleaſure, that we bear our teſtimony to its excellence, and to the comprehenſive views of thoſe enlightened ſtateſmen who framed it, by declaring that it has in practice juſtified the theory, thereby diſplaying a ſplendid example honorable to human nature and inſtructive to mankind,

freedom

freedom and order, liberty and law, can, by a wiſe policy, be made to exiſt together.

In the conduct of our government toward the republic, we have obſerved a dignified forbearance, which may have been miſinterpreted by them into puſillanimity, but which affording the ſhield of conſcious integrity, we conſider as the ſure preſage of energy and fortitude in the hour of difficulty—When that hour ſhall arrive, we truſt that the government of our country, as it has derived its origin from, ſo it will receive the efficacious ſupport of, the people; and on our part, as we value the bleſſings of ſocial order and the rights of ſelf-government, diſdaining all attempts to reconcile an attachment to the conſtitution, with a ſyſtematic oppoſition to thoſe who are choſen to adminiſter it, we pledge ourſelves, explicitly and unequivocally, to afford that ſupport to the legiſlative and executive authorities of our country, in all thoſe meaſures which by them ſhall be deemed neceſſary to defend and maintain its honor, dignity and independence.

To the GRAND JURORS *of the body of the County of* COLUMBIA, *in the State of* NEW-YORK.

GENTLEMEN,

I THANK you for this well-written and excellent addreſs. The addreſſes which I daily

I daily receive from my fellow-citizens, in greater numbers than I can poſſibly anſwer, is the cauſe of the long delay of this.

Your indignation and alarm are well founded. If there are citizens capable of being made the diſgraceful inſtruments of counteracting the meaſures of their own free government, and of proſtrating it at the feet of foreign domination, all is loſt.

The moſt infallible criterion to diſtinguiſh thoſe republics which can be ſupported and preſerved from thoſe which cannot, is the unanimity with which they reject foreign influence and reſiſt foreign hoſtility.

In contemplating our government as a free repreſentative republic, we ſhould always recollect that repreſentative government is elective government, and although the philoſophers of our age (conſcious that elective governments had from experience acquired a bad name in Europe) have been careful to give them a new one, yet we ſhall not, I truſt, be deceived by the change of a name. We know that our government, whether we call it elective or repreſentative, depends for its exiſtence on the purity of our elections, unbiaſſed by foreign influence and untainted by corruption.

Our government has indeed diſplayed an example honorable to human nature, becauſe our elections have been pure—but the

corruption

corruption of the beſt things is the worſt. If our elections become corrupt, they will exhibit a horrid example diſgraceful to human nature.

JOHN ADAMS.

From the INHABITANTS *of the County of* OTSEGO, *in the State of* NEW-YORK, *to* JOHN ADAMS, PRESIDENT *of the* UNITED STATES.

SIR,

ATTACHED by every tie that can bind us to the moſt ardent love of our country, we cannot refrain from expreſſing the great ſolicitude we feel on the ſubject of the preſent eventful period of our national affairs. Conſcious of the honeſty and juſtice of our government toward every nation in the world with which it hath had any relations, we confidently flattered ourſelves with the expectation that we ſhould have preſerved our neutrality, and the enjoyment of peace throughout the ſanguinary war which hath ſo long and doth ſtill continue to ſpread havoc and deſolation through ſeveral parts of Europe. The rapacity and aggreſſions however of one of the belligerent nations, do now very ſeriouſly threaten to diſturb that tranquillity, which the virtue and the wiſdom of our rulers have endeavored moſt

earneſtly

earnestly to preserve. We rely with great confidence on the good sense, fortitude and integrity of our fellow-citizens throughout the union, to repel every attack, both foreign and domestic, to which we may be exposed, and we do most solemnly pledge ourselves to support with cheerfulness and with promptitude, such measures for the preservation of the independence and sovereignty of our country as Congress and our rulers may in their wisdom deem expedient. The prudent but energetic regulations which you have adopted and pursued with regard to the unsuccessful negociation with the republic of France, have been, we conceive, strictly consistent with the honor and dignity of a great nation, and demonstrate in the strongest terms your unceasing regard for our common interest; and merit a continuation of our unfeigned and grateful acknowledgments. We rejoice in the prospect of unanimity on the present important occasion—One sentiment appears to pervade our land; to devote our lives and fortunes to the maintenance of our rights, as a free people. Under these impressions, we whose lots are cast on the frontiers of our country, beg leave to express our sentiments on the occasion—our pursuit being agriculture; we have no words that we expect will be more grateful to the government we love, and will not part with, but with our lives,

lives, than those of our sincere assurance, that we will submit with cheerfulness to any equal tax the wisdom of our government may lay on us for the national support; and that we will march with alacrity to any part of the Union to repel an intruder.

To the INHABITANTS *of the County of* OTSEGO, *in the State of* NEW-YORK.

GENTLEMEN,

I THANK you for your address, presented to me by your representative in Congress, Mr. Cochran.

The solicitude you feel in the present eventful period of our national affairs, is common to the government and people, to all who are attached to their country by an ardent love of it.

Your reliance on the good sense, fortitude and integrity of your fellow-citizens, I trust will not deceive you; all depends upon these virtues. If these fail us, we are lost, our constitution and administration all depend upon them. Our government without these aids, has no power at home or abroad: We have no other principle of union, or capacity of defence.

Your unfeigned acknowledgments are very obliging to me, and the clear assuran-

ces

ces of ſupport to the meaſures of government, are very encouraging to us all. Your lot on the frontiers, and your purſuits of agriculture, give a weight to your ſentiments; you may be ſuppoſed to be leſs heated by paſſion, leſs affected by prejudices, and leſs influenced by partial or local intereſts than the inhabitants of great cities.

There can be no ſtronger proof of patriotiſm, than a cheerful ſubmiſſion to any tax which the wiſdom of government may impoſe, or than a promiſe to march with alacrity, to any part of the Union to repel an intruder.

JOHN ADAMS.

From the INHABITANTS *of the County of* ONEIDA, *in the State of* NEW-YORK, *to the* PRESIDENT *of the* UNITED STATES.

SIR,

AT any other period in the political annals of our country, we might have remained ſilent, repoſing ourſelves with confidence in the adminiſtration of the government of our own choice, and evincing a tranquil but reſpectful approbation of the meaſures of that government. But, Sir, when the wide-ſpread imputation, of an alienation of the American people from their government, is

propagated

propagated and accredited abroad; when a foreign nation, which has by her agents denounced our independence, cherishes the slander, and counts upon our divisions as the means of national degradation and abasement, we have deemed it our indispensable duty to assure the Executive of our government, and proclaim to the world, that that *alienation* and *those divisions* have no place in this part of the Union. In recurring to the part, we have sought with anxious minds for just grounds of offence in the conduct of our government towards the French republic; but in this review, those grounds have been sought for in vain.

From the first dawn of the eventful revolution in France to this day, we have witnessed in the conduct of the American government, to the French nation, on the most trying occasions, amidst rude external assaults, and the more dangerous undermining influence within, an unceasing regard to justice; an inflexible adherence to the stipulations of subsisting treaties, and a sacred respect for the great land-marks of moral duty and rectitude: a conduct which we are proud, as independent Americans, to have preserved in the annals of our country, for example to future times.

Happy would it have been for America, and doubly so for distressed Europe, if cor-

O responding

responding sentiments of justice and virtue had animated the breasts of the rulers of France, and influenced the councils of that nation! But what a reverse! what a dereliction of public virtue! what a triumph of force over justice! of despotism over laws! What scenes of depravity and corruption are disclosed to astonished America!

In vain we look for a display of those transcendent virtues of which the world has witnessed in the rulers of France, so ample and repeated professions. The cause of republican government is disgraced in Europe forever; the fond expectations of the sincere advocates of reform on the other side of the Atlantic, are dashed to the ground; and the friends to the rights of man are constrained to weep for suffering humanity.

While we view with much concern, the present alarming crisis, we cannot believe the period has arrived, when Americans are to despair of their republic, and pass under a foreign yoke.

There is not to be found one community of freemen on earth, which is unsubdued by the artifices, and unsubjugated by the arms of the *all-conquering republic*.

With the fullest confidence in our government, we do not hesitate to declare, that we are prepared for any sacrifice, that the sovereignty and independence of our country may demand ; and if war muſt be the neceſſary reſort, the independent yeomanry of this country, with arms in their hands, and zeal in their hearts, will rally round their government, and appealing to the great Diſpenſer of juſtice and Arbiter of nations for the rectitude of their conduct, will cheerfully diſcharge the laſt and great duty of freemen.

To the INHABITANTS *of the County of* ONEIDA, *in the State of* NEW-YORK.

GENTLEMEN,

I THANK you for your addreſs which has been preſented to me by your repreſentative in Congreſs, Mr. Gochran.

The teſtimony you bear to the juſtice, good faith and moral rectitude of your government, and your ſatisfaction to have its conduct preſerved in the annals of our country, for an example to future times, are very full and honorable.

The cauſe of a certain ſpecies of republican government, is diſgraced in Europe forever ; yet there are other kinds better digeſted, and more adapted to the nature of man, which we may ſtill hope to ſee introduced.

When the neceſſity of controlling the paſſions of whole nations, as well as parties and [illegible]ons, by the organization and arrangement of government, ſhall be better underſtood,

ſtood, the advocates for reform may ſtill be gratified, and the friend of the rights of man ſtill rejoice in the progreſs of humanity.

JOHN ADAMS.

From the OFFICERS *of the* BRIGADE *of the City and County of* NEW-YORK *and County of* RICHMOND, *to His Excellency* JOHN ADAMS, PRESIDENT *of the* UNITED STATES.

SIR,

AMIDST the numerous teſtimonials of perſonal reſpect, and of attachment to the government, which you are daily receiving from every part of the Union, we preſumed that an expreſſion of ſimilar ſentiments from the officers of this brigade, would not be unacceptable to you.

Attached to our country by every tie of nature and affection, and to our conſtitution and government—from the ſoundeſt dictates of our judgment and underſtanding, we have ever conſidered the happineſs and proſperity of the former, as inſeparably connected with the honor and independence of the latter. While, therefore, we have, with pleaſure, beheld our government during the late war which has convulſed and deſolated the European world, purſuing with uprightneſs and integrity

integrity that syſtem of neutrality, which could alone ſecure to us the bleſſings of peace, it was with the higheſt indignation we obſerved the republic of France, under various pretences, obſtructing that peaceful ſyſtem, refuſing us our neutral rights, aſſailing our very independence as a nation— Confiding in your well known patriotiſm and abilities, we truſted that ſuch meaſures would be purſued as would reſtore to our country its violated rights, or leave its enemies without an excuſe, nor has this hope been diſappointed. The inſtructions to our envoys at that republic, have ſhewn to us, and will evince to the world, that to preſerve the peace, and to reſtore the friendſhip that once ſubſiſted between the two republics, every thing on the part of our government has been attempted, conſiſtent with thoſe ſacred duties which we owe to our rights and honor, as a free and independent people.

Impreſſed with theſe ſentiments, and with this conviction, we have thought it our duty at this eventful moment, when the independence of our country has been menaced, thus to declare, that while in common with the reſt of our fellow-citizens, we conſider peace as a bleſſing highly to be prized, and ſtudiouſly to be cultivated, yet, educated in the principles of our late glorious revolution, we are convinced that war, with all its attendant diſtreſſes, is far preferable to a ſurrender of our national freedom and independence; and that we are therefore prepared, and *will* at *all hazards*, ſupport the government of our country in ſuch meaſures as they ſhall direct, for the defence of our honor, our freedom, and our independence.

To the OFFICERS *of the* BRIGADE *of the City and County of* NEW-YORK *and County of* RICHMOND.

GENTLEMEN,

NO teſtimonals of perſonal reſpect to me, or of attachment to the government, could be more acceptable than thoſe in this addreſs, which breathe the genuine ſentiments of Americans attached to their country, by every tie of nature and affection.

I am happy, in your opinion, that thoſe who inſult and injure us, are left without excuſe, becauſe every thing on the part of our government has been attempted, conſiſtent with thoſe ſacred duties which we owe to our rights and honor, as a free and independent people.

Your opinion, that war with all its attendant diſtreſſes, is far preferable to a ſurrender of our national freedom, is undoubtedly juſt and becoming Americans; but our ſituation

is

is ſuch, that a ſurrender of our independence to thoſe who aſſail it, would only more ſurely involve us in the worſt war that could fall to our lot.

The real queſtion before us ſeems to be, whether we ſhall involve ourſelves in an unjuſt and unneceſſary war of offence againſt one nation,—Or, be involved by the fraud and violence of another, in a juſt and neceſſary war of defence.—Beſides, how many nations who have never injured, inſulted or offended us, are we to aſſiſt or contribute to deſtroy?

It is better to be prepared, as you are, at all hazards, to ſupport the government of our country in the meaſures neceſſary for the defence of our honor.

JOHN ADAMS.

NEW-JERSEY.

The MEMORIAL *of the* INHABITANTS *of the County of* BURLINGTON, *to the* PRESIDENT, *the* SENATE, *and the Houſe of* REPRESENTATIVES *of the* UNITED STATES *of* AMERICA----

RESPECTFULLY SHEWETH,

THAT deeply impreſſed by a ſenſe of the bleſſings they enjoy under the truly free and equal

equal government of the United States, they, as members of this happy and highly favored community, are determined at every hazard to maintain their rights, freedom and independence. Attached to their country and constitution, by the strongest ties of interest and affection, your memorialists declare, that as the conduct pursued by the President to preserve peace with foreign nations, merits and receives their perfect and grateful approbation, so their confidence in the wisdom and patriotism of every branch of the government being complete, they pledge themselves firmly to support every measure which may hereafter be thought necessary to secure the rights and independence of the United States.

EXTRACT *from the* ANSWER *of the* PRESIDENT, *to the* INHABITANTS *of the County of* BURLINGTON.

"GENTLEMEN,

"THERE is nothing in the conduct of our enemies more remarkable than their total contempt of the people, while they pretend to do all for the people, and of all real republican governments, while they screen themselves under some of their names and forms; while they are erecting military despotisms, under the delusive names of representative

ſentative democracies; they are demoliſhing the Pope by the moſt machiavelian maxim of one of his predeceſſors, "If the good people will be deceived, let *him* be deceived."

"The American people are unqueſtionably the beſt qualified, of any great nation in the world, by their character, habits, and all other circumſtances, for a real republican government; yet the American people are repreſented as in oppoſition, in enmity, and on the point of hoſtility againſt the government of their own inſtitution, and the adminiſtration of their own choice. If this were true, what would be the conſequence? Nothing more, nor leſs, than that they are ripe for a military deſpotiſm, under the domination of a foreign power; it is to me no wonder, that American blood boils at theſe ideas.

"Your ardent attachment to the conſtitution and government of the United States, and compleat confidence in all its departments; your firm reſolution, at every hazard, to maintain, ſupport and defend, with your lives and fortunes, every meaſure, which by your lawful repreſentatives, may be deemed neceſſary, to protect the rights, liberty and independence of the United States of America, will do you honor with all the world, and with all poſterity.

JOHN ADAMS."

The

The ADDRESS *and* MEMORIAL *of the* CITIZENS *of* NEWARK, *in the State of* NEW-JERSEY, *to the* PRESIDENT, *the* SENATE, *and the House of* REPRESENTATIVES *of the* UNITED STATES *of* AMERICA—

RESPECTFULLY SHEWETH,

THAT your memorialists view the present time as pregnant with events highly important to the peace, happiness and safety of the United States, and therefore requiring the most perfect unanimity, both in the national councils, and among every description of citizens.

The communications from our commissioners at Paris, and the instructions given to them by the President of the United States, and which are now made public, have produced a very happy effect, by convincing us that every measure, consistent with the honor, interest and independence of the United States, has been attempted by our government to effect a good understanding between us and the French republic; and we lament that, for want of a similar disposition on the part of the French republic, all those endeavors have as yet proved abortive.

Your memorialists possess the most unshaken confidence in the government, and trust that while they are pursuing just measures to produce an amicable adjustment of all

all the existing differences which at present subsist between the French republic and the United States; they will at the same time be prepared with firmness to repel all attempts that are made hostile to the peace, government and dignity of the United States.

Your memorialists are fully persuaded that the difference in opinion which has prevailed among the citizens of the United States, has been owing to delusion and misrepresentation; and that the information lately received, has led almost all our citizens to a determination to rally round the constitution, and to defend the same with our lives and fortunes.

To the CITIZENS *of* NEWARK, *in the State of* NEW-JERSEY.

GENTLEMEN,

THE present period of universal effervescence through the world, is indeed pregnant with events highly important to the safety of all nations: that nation must be unconnected with the rest of mankind, which can depend upon a total exemption from its feelings, and sympathies: the United States are so largely and extensively connected, that they ought to have been sooner apprized of the necessity of unanimity in council, and among the citizens at large.

I rejoice

I rejoice with you in any event which may have produced the happy effect of uniting the people in supporting their own government, and opposing the unreasonable dispositions of others.

I thank you for your declaration of unshaken confidence in the government, and for your advice, to be prepared with firmness, to repel all attempts that are made, against the peace, government and dignity of the United States; but I know of no further measures that can be pursued to produce an amicable adjustment of differences with the French republic.

The delusions and misrepresentations, which have misled so many citizens, are very serious evils and must be discountenanced by authority, as well as by the citizens at large, or they will soon produce all kinds of calamities in this country.

If the late information has led almost all our citizens to a determination to rally round the constitution, and defend it with their lives and fortunes, I congratulate you most sincerely on this happy event, so auspicious to the safety, greatness and glory of our country.

JOHN ADAMS.

To JOHN ADAMS, PRESIDENT *of the* UNITED STATES.

SIR,

THE inhabitants of Bridgeton, in the county of Cumberland, New-Jerſey, being convened in public meeting, and having taken into conſideration the preſent critical ſituation of our national affairs, are deſirous of making known to you their unanimous opinion on the ſubject.

Although we diſapprove of addreſſes on ordinary occurrences, which reſpect the *interior* concerns, or domeſtic adminiſtration of our national government,as we apprehend that our repreſentative bodies and conſtituted authorities, are the proper conſtitutional organs for expreſſing the political ſentiment and *will* of the people ; yet, on the preſent extraordinary occaſion, reſpecting our *exterior* intercourſe with the French nation, in which they appear evidently to be influenced and encouraged, in their inſults on our national character, and depredations on our commerce, by an erroneous opinion, that there exiſts a diviſion, between the adminiſtrators of the government and the people of this country ; we eſteem it an incumbent duty, to teſtify our *entire* approbation of your conduct, and full confidence in your adminiſtration, more eſpecially in relation to the republic of France.

P We

We have obſerved with much pleaſure and ſatisfaction, that the wiſe and prudent meaſures adopted by your predeceſſor, to preſerve and ſupport a fair and impartial neutrality with the belligerent powers of Europe, and to protect the commerce of our country, have been ſteadily purſued by you. And though we firmly believe that the preſent miſunderſtanding between the republics of France and America, cannot fairly be imputed to any unjuſtifiable conduct on the part of the latter, we, nevertheleſs, entirely approve of the inſtructions given to our envoys to the French republic, and the conciliatory and pacific endeavors which have been uſed, for accommodating the differences, and reſtoring a friendly intercourſe and good underſtanding with that government.

While we expreſs a juſt indignation at the diſgraceful treatment of our diplomatic agents by the French Directory, we ſincerely regret that the deſirable objects of their embaſſy, have hitherto proved unattainable. And ſhould it become neceſſary to repel, by force, the unjuſt aggreſſions of any foreign nation whatever, we are determined, at all events, to ſupport the Executive, and defend the honor, intereſt, and independence, of our country.

To

To the INHABITANTS *of* BRIDGETON, *in the County of* CUMBERLAND, *in the State of* NEW-JERSEY.

GENTLEMEN,

TO you who disapprove of addresses of compliment in general, and of the interposition of constituents in the ordinary course of national affairs, my thanks are more particularly due, for the part you have taken at this extraordinary crisis.

In preparing the project of a treaty to be proposed by Congress to France, in the year 1776, fully apprized of the importance of neutrality, I prescribed to myself as a rule, to admit nothing which could compromise the United States in any future wars of Europe—In the negociations of peace in 1782, I saw stronger reasons than ever before, in favor of that maxim.

The wise and prudent measures adopted by my predecessor, to preserve and support a fair and impartial neutrality, with the belligerent powers of Europe, coinciding with my own opinions and principles, more ancient than the birth of the United States, could not but be heartily approved and supported by me, during his whole administration, and steadily pursued until this time. It was, however, no part of the system of my predecessor, nor is it any article of my creed, that neutrality should be purchased

with

with bribes, by the ſacrifice of our ſovereignty, and the abandonment of our independence, by the ſurrender of our moral character, by tarniſhing our honor, by violations of public faith, or by any means humiliating to our own national pride, or diſgraceful in the eyes of the world; nor will I be the inſtrument of procuring it on ſuch terms.

I thank you, gentlemen, for your candid approbation, and your noble aſſurances of ſupport.

JOHN ADAMS.

From the INHABITANTS *of the Townſhips of* WINDSOR *and* MONTGOMERY, *and the Towns of* PRINCETON *and* KINGSTON, *to the* PRESIDENT, *the* SENATE, *and Houſe of* REPRESENTATIVES *of the* UNITED STATES.

LEGISLATORS, AND RULERS OF AMERICA,

AT an intereſting criſis, like the preſent, you will naturally be ſolicitous to be ſincerely poſſeſſed of the public ſentiment, and to know to what point you may depend on the cheerful and zealous co-operation and aid of every citizen, in the energetic meaſures which you may find it neceſſary to adopt for the public good.

Although

Although, claiming an equality with you, in your private and individual capacities, as your fellow-citizens—in your reprefentative functions we venerate you as the organs, and refpect in your perfons the majefty of the laws. We prefume not, under the form of refolutions or inftructions, to dictate to thofe to whom we have entrufted the right of judging, and whofe fituation afford them the beft means of forming their decifions with wifdom and an equal regard to the general interefts. We have affembled at this important moment, only to pledge to you our loyalty and fidelity. We eftimate, at its juft value, the precious liberty which we enjoy; and we feel, with an honeft pride, that national dignity, and that felf refpect which the freeft people on earth ought to feel. Americans have broken the yoke of one tyrant, and they will not become the tributaries of another.

We have feen with indignation the depredations committed on our lawful commerce, and the repeated infults offered to our government, whilft it has fought nothing but peace, on juft and equitable terms. We have feen, with the difdainful fentiments that become freemen, the late efforts to reduce us to the dependent and degraded ftate of Milan, or Genoa, or to enflave and difmember us like the miferable republic of Venice. We have feen, with mingled emo-

 tions

tions of resentment and contempt, the insolent proposals to exact from us an enormous and incalculable tribute, not only to aid the national interests of France, which though less humiliating, would still be intolerable to a free people, but to maintain the profligacy and vice of her individual, miserable agents—a condition below infamy itself.

LEGISLATORS! RULERS!

We pledge to you our lives, our fortunes, and our sacred honor; we will cheerfully submit to every pecuniary burthen you may think it necessary to impose, for the safety and defence of the republic; and the militia of New-Jersey, will, as they have always done, fly at your command, either to repel the invasion of foreign enemies, or to crush the villany of domestic traitors. We pray for peace, while it can be preserved on honorable terms; but trusting in heaven, in our courage, and the justice of our cause, we cannot fear the insolence of any nation. The calamities of war we deprecate; but we hold no calamity to be so great as that of dependence on a foreign power; and no calculation can be made of national honor, except by those who deserve to be *slaves*. A people, who can so far forget themselves, must soon submit to exactions, calculated, not on their ability to pay, but on the wants, the will, and the vices of their tyrants. Our confidence in the wisdom and integrity of the

the Executive of the United States, has always been unſhaken and entire, and we find it daily augmented by the developement of events. If diviſions have weakened the legiſlature, and tempted the avarice or ambition of foreign powers to form the moſt criminal expectations, we truſt, hereafter, that unanimity and energy will defeat their unwarrantable views. As far as depends on us, we will refute the ſlanders that have repreſented us as a people divided from our government; we will diſappoint thoſe inſidious intriguers who are inceſſantly ſtriving to create a ſeparation, that they may have a pretence for intermeddling in our domeſtic policy; and at length an opportunity of enſlaving us, as they have done ſo many other ſtates, by taking under their protection a turbulent faction in the name of the people.

In proportion as the ſincerity and humanity of the American people have led them to ſhew a forbearance, in the purſuit of peace, which has been miſconſtrued into puſillanimity or a mercenary dereliction of the ſolid intereſts and glory of their country, will they, when rouſed by the injuſtice of their enemies, diſplay a noble firmneſs and enterprize in its defence.

Although it belongs not to us to dictate meaſures to government, it is a privilege which we truſt will not be unacceptable to

you

you in this trying juncture, to declare our warm and unequivocal approbation of the wise and temperate system which has hitherto been pursued with regard to our foreign relations, and our undiminished confidence in those who preside over the affairs of the nation with so much wisdom and prudence. We are prepared for every event. If you should deem it necessary to impose a restraint upon foreign commerce, we will cheerfully forego the conveniences of living, which commerce yields. If, on the other hand, you resolve to claim your rights and bravely to defend them, we make not indeed any boastful professions of chaining victory to our arms, but we fear not to meet either in the field or on the ocean, those who have been accustomed to boast.

That the Eternal, who presides in secret over the fate of empires, may preserve the American people, and ever have your Excellency, and you the honorable members of the Senate and the House of Representatives, in his gracious and powerful protection, is the fervent prayer of your respectful fellow-citizens, and the obedient subjects of the laws, the inhabitants and freeholders of the precincts of Princeton and Kingston, and the townships of Montgomery and Windsor, in the State of New-Jersey.

To

To the INHABITANTS *of the Townſhips of* WINDSOR *and* MONTGOMERY, *and the Towns of* PRINCETON *and* KINGSTON.

GENTLEMEN,

YOUR dutiful and loyal addreſs to the Preſident, Senate, and Houſe of Repreſentatives, was preſented in its ſeaſon, with expreſs information that no anſwer was expected; although for this reaſon, I have hitherto neglected to anſwer it, I muſt ſay, that no addreſs has deſerved or received a more reſpectful and affectionate attention.

If the veneration you profeſs, for the repreſentatives of the nation, and the organs of the public judgment and will, are not juſt, where is, or can be the object of public confidence? Where can be found the rule of action for the citizen? There can be no alternative between this and anarchy:—every man, the fooliſh as well as the wiſe, the wicked as well as the juſt, doing what is right in his own eyes; and we know that in ſuch a caſe, the *bad* being under no reſtraint of conſcience, will have the advantage of the *good*, who can permit themſelves to do no wrong. The very modern hiſtory of the laſt twelve years, has abundantly illuſtrated the proverb, that anarchy does more miſchief in one night than even tyranny itſelf in ten years; what is the difference then between anarchy and good government?

The

The pledge of your fidelity is received with pleaſure; the eſtimate of the precious liberty you enjoy, is candid and honorable; the honeſt pride you feel in the national dignity, is a bulwark of defence and ſafety to the ſtate; the depredations committed on our commerce, the cruelties to our ſeamen, the inſults to our government, the contempt of our ambaſſadors, could have originated in nothing but a fixed opinion that the United States were like the rotten republics of Europe, ropes of ſand, decayed timbers of old ſhips, to be ſhaken to atoms by the ſmalleſt agitation.

The pledge of your lives, fortunes and your ſacred honor, ought to convince that our republic is ſtill ſound; domeſtic traitors will be found to be very few; truſting in Heaven, in your own courage and the juſtice of your cauſe, you need not fear any inſolent menaces.

Calculations of the value of national honor, in Eagles, Dollars and Cents, have been lately found by the republics of Europe, the moſt extravagant and fatal, of all ſpeculations, and the ſureſt road to bankruptcy and ruin. Wills, wants and vices, have been found to exceed all calculations. Your confidence in the executive authority deſerves my thanks—unanimity and energy are taking place of diviſions every where, and will defeat

defeat the unwarrantable projects against us. Insidious intriguers will soon find no turbulent faction to take under their protection.

I thank you for the excellent temper, principles and sentiments displayed in this address, and join you sincerely in prayers to the Eternal, who presides over the fates of empires, that he may preserve the American people.

JOHN ADAMS.

From the CITIZENS *of the Townships of* AMWELL, READINGTON, *and* KINGWOOD, *to the* PRESIDENT *of the* UNITED STATES.

SIR,

WE should do violence to the respect and loyalty we possess for our first magistrate, and the attachment, love and veneration which we entertain for our constitution and cherish for our country, were we to remain silent when our honor is insulted, our interests injured and our national rights violated; we profess, Sir, that we once were attached to the French nation, and anxiously wished that they might accomplish the *avowed* object of their revolution; but, Sir, we never will permit our zeal for any nation to induce us to lose sight of the honor, interest, dignity and freedom of our own country. We have maturely considered the attempts you

you have made to preserve an honorable peace with the French republic, and we have with pain seen their effect. We approve of and admire the pacific disposition, the wisdom, the dignified love of country and the liberal policy discoverable in your instructions to our envoys extraordinary; and we most heartily despise the corrupt, the servile, and the tributary conditions, offered to us by the agents of the Directory. Sir, we are not divided from our government—we highly approve of the administration of it—and we will with our property and services, support it, and every act of our constituted authorities, in defiance of the threats or power of any nation on earth.

To the CITIZENS *of the Townships of* AMWELL, READINGTON, *and* KINGWOOD.

GENTLEMEN,

THE respect you profess for your first magistrate is obliging to him, and your attachment, love and veneration for your constitution and country, will be amiable in the eyes of all men.

The attachment you profess for the French nation was common to you, and to America in general; but never was the attachment of one nation to another so wantonly, capriciously, so insolently despised and

and thrown away. All great things have begun in contempt—the Roman empire—the French republic—and to rise infinitely higher than both for an example, the Christian religion itself might be cited: Our American world exhibits another instance—but mark the issue;—this contempt will be changed into respect and admiration, and I hope to live to see the time and to rejoice with you in it.

JOHN ADAMS.

From the whole of the SOLDIER CITIZENS *of* NEW-JERSEY, *to the* PRESIDENT *of the* UNITED STATES.

SIR,

THE Commander in Chief, the General Officers, the General Staff and Field-Officers of the militia of the State of New-Jersey, feel, in common with their numerous fellow-citizens, who have addressed you in the present critical situation of our nation, and most cordially join them in expressing to you their high approbation of your conduct in the management of its foreign concerns, and their indignation at the insult offered to the honor and independence of the American people.

We come not, Sir, to dictate—whether peace can be preserved with the safety of our national dignity, or whether an appeal is to be made to arms, are queſtions entruſted to thoſe in whoſe patriotiſm we confide, and according to their deciſion we ſhall always be prepared to act. But, Sir, at this eventful period, we deem it our duty, and we feel it a pleaſure, reſpectfully to approach our Commander in Chief, and to make him a ſolemn proffer of our lives and fortunes in the ſervice of our country.

It is not, Sir, for ſoldiers to boaſt: but we know the troops whom we have the honor to command—we have been eye-witneſſes to their ardent zeal in the cauſe of freedom---we have been their companions in many toils and many ſufferings, and if our beloved country calls, we ſhall again caſt the eye of confidence along their embattled ranks.

Let our enemies flatter themſelves that we are a divided people.—In New-Jerſey, Sir, with the exception of a few *degraded* and a few *deluded* characters, to whoſe perſons, and to whoſe ſervices the invading foe ſhall be welcome, from the moment of their arrival, and whom we engage to convey in ſafety to their lines—In New-Jerſey, Sir, there is but *one voice*—and that is the voice of confidence in the Federal Government---the voice of perfect ſatisfaction with your adminiſtration of it --and the voice of firmneſs and determination to ſupport the laws

and

and constitution, the honor and dignity of the United States; and, Sir, for the defence of these, we do this day, in the presence of the God of armies, and in firm reliance on his protection, solemnly pledge to you, our lives, our fortunes and our sacred honor.

To the SOLDIER CITIZENS *of* NEW-JERSEY.

GENTLEMEN,

AMONG all the numerous addresses which have been presented to me, in the present critical situation of our nation, there has been none which has done me more honor, none animated with a more glowing love of our country, or expressive of sentiments more determined and magnanimous. The submission you avow to the civil authority, an indispensable principle in the character of warriors in a free government, at the same moment when you make a solemn proffer of your lives and fortunes in the service of your country, is highly honorable to your dispositions as citizens and soldiers, and proves you perfectly qualified for the duties of both characters.

Officers and soldiers of New-Jersey, have as little occasion as they have disposition to boast. Their country has long boasted of their ardent zeal in the cause of freedom, and their invincible intrepidity in the day of battle.

Your

Your voice of confidence and ſatisfaction, of firmneſs and determination to ſupport the laws and conſtitution of the United States, has a charm in it irreſiſtible to the feelings of every American boſom; but, when in the preſence of the God of armies, and in firm reliance on his protection, you ſolemnly pledge your lives and fortunes, and your ſacred honor; you have recorded words which ought to be indelibly imprinted in the memory of every American youth. With theſe ſentiments in the hearts, and this language in the mouths of Americans in general, the greateſt nation may menace at its pleaſure, and the degraded and the deluded characters may tremble, leſt they ſhould be condemned to the ſevereſt puniſhment an American can ſuffer---that of being conveyed in ſafety within the lines of an invading enemy.

JOHN ADAMS.

To the PRESIDENT *of the* UNITED STATES.

SIR,

THE ſtudents of the College of New-Jerſey, awfully impreſſed by the threatening clouds which obſcure our political horrizon, and well aware of the importance of united and vigorous exertions, would offer their feeble, though hearty concurrence, in applauding

applauding your administration, and supporting the energy of government.

We deem it the duty of every American attached to the freedom and independence of his country, to oppose the aggressions of foreign power; nor is it less incumbent on those who, though young in years and wisdom, anticipate a period, when they shall be admitted to the privilege of citizenship, zealously to defend their precious inheritance. We hope to manifest to the world, when the rules of our institution will permit, that the youth of Nassau will glory in defending the independence of their fathers.

The national honor of our country, we esteem of incalculable value—Our lives we estimate worthy of preservation only as we enjoy the independence of freemen. We view, with the ardent resentments of youth, the encroachments of foreign nations on our rights. We contemplate, with impatience, their lawless depredations. In common with our countrymen, we lament the necessity of military operations; yet, urged upon them involuntarily, we confidently trust in Heaven, that the result will be favorable to the cause of freedom and humanity. Our grief arises not from pusillanimity; it is the offspring of love to our country. Though we dare brave the intrepid attack of the hostile army, we foresee, with regret, the multiplied calamities that muſt reſult from the conflict.

Although but juſt ariſen from our cradles, when the French nation broke the ſceptre of deſpotiſm, we, Sir, in common with our fathers, caught the flame of enthuſiaſm, at the proſpect of a people enſlaved for ages, by a ſucceſſion of tyrants, at once claiming their indefeaſible rights, and nobly daring to aſſert their freedom. We fondly hoped, that the ſpirit which created, would conduct the revolution. In this hope we have been diſappointed. We have ſeen the French nation laying aſide their firſt principles of juſtice, and aiming at univerſal empire. We have ſeen them, not ſatisfied with ſubjugating or ravaging Europe, croſs the Atlantic, inſultingly trample on the rights of our neutrality, and deſpiſe the faith of the moſt ſolemn compacts. We have ſeen miniſters ſent by our Executive to accommodate differences. We have ſeen thoſe miniſters inſulted, and their friendly offers rejected. At ſuch conduct, we truſt, every American feels the warmeſt ſentiments of indignation.

We regard it as a ſingular mercy of Heaven to our country, at this important criſis, and as one of the ſureſt pledges of our political ſecurity, that you are placed at the helm of our affairs. We conſider it,

at

at the ſame time, as the reward of your well-tried patriotiſm and unſhaken firmneſs.

While therefore, Sir, we expreſs our higheſt approbation of the conduct of the Executive of the United States, in the attempts to negociate with the French republic, we would alſo, with ardor, and we truſt with the modeſty which becomes our years, declare our confidence in the conſtituted authorities of our country. The choice of the people, we know, will defend their rights and privileges. To us there appears no mean of averting the ſtorm; but we declare we are ready to dedicate our lives to fatigues and dangers in braving it.

May you long continue to watch over the ſafety and order of the community, and may our fellow-citizens never ceaſe to teſtify their livelieſt gratitude for the eminent ſervices you have rendered them.

To the STUDENTS *of* NEW-JERSEY COLLEGE.

GENTLEMEN,

I THANK you for your well-judged and well-penned addreſs, which has been preſented to me by one of your ſenators in Congreſs, from New-Jerſey, Mr. Stockton.

To an high-ſpirited youth, poſſeſſed of that ſelf-reſpect and ſelf-eſteem, which is inſepa-

rable

rable from conſcious innocence and rectitude, whoſe bodies are not enervated by irregularities of life; whoſe minds are not weakened by diſſipation or habits of luxury; whoſe natural ſentiments are improved and fortified by claſſical ſtudies, the aggreſſions of a foreign power muſt be diſguſting and odious: on theſe facts alone, I could anſwer for the youth of Naſſau, that they will glory in defending the independence of their fathers.

The honor of your country, you cannot eſtimate too highly; reputation is of as much importance to nations, in proportion, as to individuals; honor is an higher intereſt than reputation; the man, or the nation, without attachment to reputation or honor, is undone:---What is animal life, or national exiſtence, without either?

The regret with which you view the encroachments of foreign nations, the impatience with which you contemplate their lawleſs depredations, are perfectly natural, and do honor to your characters.

If regrets would avert the neceſſity of military operations, it would be well to indulge them; but, if the entire proſperity of of a ſtate depends upon the diſcipline of its armies, a maxim much reſpected by your fathers, you may hereafter be convinced that the cauſe of your country and of mankind

kind may be promoted by means, which, from love to your country and a fear to ſet at defiance the laws of nature, you now ſee cauſe to regret.

The flame of enthuſiaſm which you, in common with your fathers, caught at the French revolution, could have been enkindled only by the innocence of your hearts and the purity of your intentions. Let me, however, my amiable and accompliſhed young friends, entreat you to ſtudy the hiſtory of that revolution; the hiſtory of France during the periods of the League and the Fronde, and the hiſtory of England from 1640 to 1660. In theſe ſtudies you may perhaps find a ſolution of your diſappointment in your hopes that the ſpirit which created, would conduct the revolution: you may find that the good intended by fair characters, from the beginning, was defeated by Borgias and Catalines; that theſe fair characters themſelves were inexperienced in freedom, and had very little reading in the ſcience of government; that they were altogether inadequate to the cauſe they embraced, and the enterprize in which they embarked. You may find that the moral principles, ſanctified and ſanctioned by religion, are the only bond of union, the only ground of confidence of the people in one another, of the people in the government, and the government in the people. Avarice,

rice, ambition and pleaſure, can never be the foundations of reformations or revolutions for the better. Theſe paſſions have dictated the aim at univerſal domination; trampled on the rights of neutrality, deſpiſed the faith of ſolemn compact, inſulted ambaſſadors, and rejected offers of friendſhip.

It is to me a flattering idea, that you place any of your hopes of political ſecurity in me---mine are placed in your fathers and you; and my advice to both is, to place your confidence, under the favor of Heaven, in yourſelves.

Your approbation of the conduct of government, and confidence in its authorities, are very acceptable: If the choice of the people will not defend their rights, who will? To me there appears no mean of averting the ſtorm, and, in my opinion, we muſt all be ready to dedicate ourſelves to fatigues and dangers.

JOHN ADAMS.

PENNSYLVANIA.

To the PRESIDENT *of the* UNITED STATES.

SIR,

AT a moment when dangers threaten the peace and proſperity of the United States, when

when foreign insolence and rapine have deeply wounded our national honor, and injured our lawful commerce; it is presumed the Mayor, Aldermen and Citizens of the city of Philadelphia will not be unwelcome--- when they come forward to assure you of their perfect approbation of your administration, and their entire confidence in your wisdom, integrity and patriotism. While we admire the prudence and moderation with which our government has received the unprovoked aggressions of France, and the sincerity and equity of your endeavors to conciliate her friendship, we feel the independent pride of Americans in your dignity and firmness. As we are satisfied that nothing has been wanting on your part to preserve to us the blessings of peace and safety, we prepare to meet with fortitude the consequences that may follow the failure of your exertions. Confident that our government has been just and impartial in her dealings with all nations, and grateful for the happiness and prosperity we have enjoyed under it in the days of tranquillity, we do not hesitate to promise it our utmost assistance in the time of difficulty and need.

Presiding over the counsels of your country in a most eventful crisis, we hope and trust you will find a fixed and energetic support in the people of America. Permit us to congratulate you on the prospect of unanimity

nimity that now presents itself to the hopes of every American, and on the spirit of independent patriotism that is rapidly rising into active exertion---and to offer a sincere prayer that while you continue to serve your country with wisdom and fidelity, you may never find her ungrateful.

To the MAYOR, ALDERMEN *and* CITIZENS *of the City of* PHILADELPHIA.

GENTLEMEN,

NEVER, as I can recollect, were any class of my fellow-citizens more welcome to me, on any occasion, than the Mayor, Aldermen and Citizens of the city of Philadelphia upon this.

At a time, when all the old republics of Europe are crumbling into dust, and others forming, whose destinies are dubious; when the monarchies of the old world are some of them are fallen, and others trembling to their foundations; when our own infant republic has scarcely had time to cement its strength or decide its own practicable form; when these agitations of the human species have affected our people, and produced a spirit of party which scruples not to go all lengths of profligacy, falsehood and malignity in defaming our government; your approbation and confidence are to me a great consolation.

consolation. Under your immediate observation and inspection, the principal operations of the government are directed; and to you, both characters and conduct must be intimately known.

I am but one of the American people, and my fate and fortune must be decided with theirs. As far as the forces of nature may remain to me, I will not be wanting in my duties to them, nor will I harbor a suspicion that they will fail to afford me all necessary aid and support.

While, with the greatest pleasure, I reciprocate your congratulations on the prospect of unanimity that now presents itself to the hopes of every American, and on that spirit of patriotism and independence that is rising into active exertion in opposition to seduction, domination and rapine, I offer a sincere prayer that the citizens of Philadelphia may persevere in the virtuous course and maintain the honorable character of their ancestors, and be protected from every calamity physical, moral and political.

JOHN ADAMS.

To the CITIZENS *of* PHILADELPHIA, *the* *District of* SOUTHWARK, *and the* NORTHERN LIBERTIES.

GENTLEMEN,

MANY of the nations of the earth, disgusted with their present governments, seem determined to dissolve them, without knowing what other forms to substitute in their places. An ignorance, with all the cruel intolerance of the most bloody superstitions that ever have existed, is imposing its absurd dogmas by the sword, without the smallest attention to that emulation universal in the human heart, which is a great spring of generous action when wisely regulated, but the never-failing source of anarchy and tyranny when uncontroled by the constitution of the state. As the United States are a part of the society of mankind, and are closely connected with several nations now struggling in arms, the present period is indeed pregnant with events of the highest importance to their happiness and safety.

In such a state of things, your implicit approbation of the general system, and the particular measures of the government; your generous feelings of resentment at the wrongs and offences committed against it, and at the menaces of others still more intolerable; your candid acknowledgment of the blessings you enjoy under its free and equal

equal constitution; your determination at every hazard to maintain your freedom and independence, and to support the measures which may be thought necessary to support the constitution, freedom and independence of the United States; do you great honor as patriots and citizens; and your communication of these spirited sentiments to me, deserves my best thanks.

JOHN ADAMS.

To JOHN ADAMS, PRESIDENT *of the* UNITED STATES.

SIR,

AT a period so interesting to the United States, permit us to believe that an address from the Youth of Philadelphia, anxious to preserve the honor and independence of their country, will not be unwelcome to their chief magistrate.

Actuated by the same principles on which our forefathers achieved their independence, the recent attempts of a foreign power to derogate from the dignity and rights of our country, awaken our liveliest sensibility, and our strongest indignation.

The Executive of the United States, filled with a spirit of friendship towards the whole world, has resorted to every just and honorable mean of conciliating the affections of the

not correſpond with my earneſt wiſhes, and I ſhould be obliged, to act with you, as with your anceſtors, in defence of the honor and independence of our country, I ſincerely wiſh that none of you may ever have your conſtancy of mind and ſtrength of body put to ſo ſevere a trial, as to be compelled again in your advanced age to the contemplation and near proſpect, of any war of offence or defence.

It would neither be conſiſtent with my character, nor yours, on this occaſion, to read leſſons to gentlemen of your education, conduct and character; if, however, I might be indulged the privilege of a father, I ſhould, with the tendereſt affections, recommend to your ſerious and conſtant conſideration, that ſcience and morals are the great pillars on which this country has been raiſed to its preſent population, opulence and proſperity, and that theſe alone, can advance, ſupport and preſerve it.

Without wiſhing to damp the ardor of curioſity, or influence the freedom of inquiry, I will hazard a prediction that after the moſt induſtrious and impartial reſearches, the longeſt liver of you all, will find no principles, inſtitutions, or ſyſtems of education, more fit, in general, to be tranſmitted to your poſterity, than thoſe you have received from your anceſtors.

No

No profpect or fpectacle, could excite a ftronger fenfibility in my bofom, than this which now prefents itfelf before me. I wifh you all the pure joys, the fanguine hopes, and bright profpects, which are decent at your age, and that your lives may be long, honorable and profperous, in the conftant practice of benevolence to men, and reverence to the Divinity, in a country perfevering in liberty, and increafing in virtue, power and glory.

The fentiments of this addrefs, every where expreffed in language as chafte and modeft, as it is elegant and mafterly, which would do honor to the youth of any country, have raifed a monument to your fame, more durable than brafs or marble.—The youth of all America muft exult in this early fample, at the feat of government, of their talents, genius and virtues.

America, and the world, will look to our youth, as one of our firmeft bulwarks. The generous claim which you now prefent of fharing in the difficulty, danger and glory of our defence, is to me and to your country, a fure and pleafing pledge, that your birth-rights will never be ignobly bartered or furrendered : But that you will in your turn, tranfmit to future generations the fair inheritance, obtained by the unconquerable fpirit of your fathers.

JOHN ADAMS.

From

From the INHABITANTS *of the County of* LANCASTER, *to the* PRESIDENT *of the* UNITED STATES.

SIR,

AT this alarming crisis in our political existence, we approach you, Sir, to express our cordial approbation of the measures adopted by the Executive for the preservation of the neutrality and peace of our country. The firm reliance we have had on your patriotism and attachment to the genuine principles of liberty, as guaranteed to us by our excellent constitution, is, if possible, strengthened and enlarged by a policy so congenial with the character of the chief magistrate of a free people.

Whatever may be the real or imaginary pretensions of an ally which derogates from a state of amity, the distinction and honor of the aggressing nation, require an investigation of the supposed infractions of friendship upon the basis of equality A demand of a preliminary submission acknowledging the commission of an offence—a stipulation for pecuniary compensation anterior to the discussion of the causes of discord, are debasements of national dignity, totally incompatible with the sovereignty and independence of a nation.

Holding these to be self-evident truths, which men nursed in the bosom of freedom,

can

can by no means permit to be gainſaid—we feel ourſelves forcibly drawn to acknowledge to you, a thankfulneſs for the earneſt endeavors you have uſed in your diplomatic intercourſe to cultivate and nouriſh harmony with the French republic: For the ſincere, candid and unequivocal manner with which you have diſplayed the fair and upright principles of the United States in the propoſed negociation with that republic: And for your nomination (as commiſſioners to France) of three of our fellow-citizens, whoſe energy of mind and love of country, have enabled them to reſiſt terms of conciliation degrading to the national character and diſhonorable to the government.

If unhappily the United States be driven into hoſtility by the injuſtice and inſatiate ambition of the French republic, we truſt that that benign Being, whoſe aid in our keeneſt diſtreſſes we have ſo frequently experienced, will again become auxiliary to the arms of freemen, honeſtly contending for the liberty and independence of their country. We aſſure you, Sir, for ourſelves perſonally, that, in ſuch a conflict, no conſiderations of eaſe to our eſtates or ſafety to our perſons, ſhall deter us from the exertion of every power we poſſeſs in the ſupport of government.

We fervently implore the Supreme Diſpoſer of events, to continue your health of

body,

body, fortitude of mind, and mature wisdom, that you may be empowered in your arduous ſtation to lead us through this perilous era, with honor to yourſelf, and an acceſſion of glory to the American name.

To the INHABITANTS *of the County of* LANCASTER.

GENTLEMEN,

THIS reſpectful and affectionate addreſs, from the wealthy, induſtrious and independent proprietors of the county of Lancaſter, is as honorable, as it is agreeable to me, and is returned with my hearty thanks.

The attention you have given to a demand of a preliminary ſubmiſſion, acknowledging the commiſſion of offence, requires an obſervation on my part. The conſtitution of the United States makes it my duty to communicate to Congreſs, from time to time, information of the ſtate of the Union, and to recommend to their conſideration, meaſures which appear to me neceſſary or expedient. While in diſcharge of this duty, I ſubmit, with entire reſignation, to the reſponſibility eſtabliſhed in the conſtitution, I hold myſelf accountable to no crowned head, or Executive Directory, or other foreign power on earth, for the communications which my duty obliges me to make; yet to you, my fellow-citizens, I will freely ſay,

ſay, that, in the caſe alluded to, the honor done, the publicity and ſolemnity given to the audience of leave, to a diſgraced miniſter, recalled in diſpleaſure for miſconduct, was a ſtudied inſult to the government of my country.

The obſervations made by me, were mild and moderate, in a degree far beyond what the provocation would have juſtified; and if the American people, or their government, could have borne it without reſentment, offered as it was in the face of all the world, they muſt have been fit to be the tributary dupes they have ſince been ſo cooly invited to become.

As I know not where a better choice of envoys could have been made, I thank you for your approbation of their appointment, and applauſe of their conduct.

In return for your prayers, for my health and fortitude, I offer mine for the citizens of Lancaſter in particular, and the United States in general.

JOHN ADAMS.

To the PRESIDENT *of the* UNITED STATES.

SIR,

WHILE the citizens of America, in every part of the Union, are addreſſing you with

with expreſſions of affection and tenders of their ſervices, at this moſt important criſis; we, the inhabitants of Carliſle and its vicinity, inſpired by the ſame love of our country, and attachment to its beſt intereſts, deſire alſo to expreſs our ſentiments reſpecting the affairs of our nation, with becoming freedom. Inheriting liberty as a birthright, and riſing above the degrading ſpirit of colonial dependence, we not only have a character already eſtabliſhed as freemen and defenders of our country, but we are reſolved to maintain that character at every hazard.

Under a government of our own choice, and the auſpices of a wiſe and juſt adminiſtration, we have enjoyed for a number of years, as great a ſhare of national proſperity and happineſs, as has perhaps ever fallen to the lot of any people. Having eſtabliſhed a free government, on the ſolid baſis of the general will, we could not but grant that other nations had a right to regulate and manage their own internal concerns in like manner. In their endeavors to this end, we conceived we ought not to interfere, and we wiſhed to enjoy the bleſſings of neutrality and peace; diſcharging at the ſame time all the obligations we might be under to any European power, with the utmoſt good faith and impartiality.

The meaſures that have been purſued by the Executive from time to time, to maintain

tain such a ſtate of things, and to preſerve us from the evils of war and national degradation, have met and ſtill meet with our hearty approbation. The appointment of envoys extraordinary, for the adjuſtment of all our differences with France, and the ample powers with which they were veſted for this end, manifeſted the ſincereſt diſpoſition for peace and juſtice, and the happineſs of both nations; nor can we conſider the treatment which thoſe envoys have received, the demands that have been made of us, and the threats denounced againſt us if we will not comply with their wiſhes, without feeling as Americans ought to feel, and reſolving that we will cheerfully concur in the ſupport of all meaſures which ſhall appear neceſſary for the national defence, and the maintenance of that freedom and independence which we hold moſt dear.

While we join with you in humbly ſoliciting the ſmiles of Divine Providence on our national affairs, and the bleſſings of genuine freedom, accept, Sir, of our ſincere prayers for your perſonal happineſs.

To the CITIZENS *of the Borough of* CARLISLE *and its vicinity.*

GENTLEMEN,

NOTHING could be more obliging to me or faithful to the public than the unanimous

imous resolutions and address of the citizens of Carlisle, which have been presented to me by one of your senators in Congress, Mr. Bingham.

When you declare your resolution to maintain your established character, as freemen and members of an independent nation, as your birthright, the world will applaud your wisdom, as well as virtue. When you acknowledge that under a government of your choice, and the auspices of a wise and just administration, you have enjoyed as great a share of national prosperity and happiness, as has perhaps ever fallen to the lot of any people, you do great honor to your government. Nevertheless, I presume there is not a city or a village in the Sixteen States that can contradict you: If there is one, I hope it will assemble and declare it.

When you acknowledge the rights of nations to regulate their own internal concerns, on the solid basis of the general will, you recognize one of the highest prerogatives of man. Like all other prerogatives, however, it ought always to be exerted with wisdom and integrity for the general good; never for the purposes of private ambition, party views or foreign intrigues.

When you approve the measures of the general government, you deserve its thanks —and your feelings of the unworthy return of of insults and menaces, are the feelings of nature approved by reason and justified by the public voice.

In your humble supplications for the smiles of Providence on our national affairs and the blessings of genuine freedom, you will be joined by all good men. Your prayers for my personal happiness are most affecting to me.

JOHN ADAMS.

From the INHABITANTS *of* BERKS *County, to the* PRESIDENT *of the* UNITED STATES.

SIR,

THE interesting crisis to which the United States are at last driven by the rapacity, wickedness, and ambition of the French government, calls loudly and explicitly upon us to unite in defence of our country; and by displaying that unanimity to the world, to convince our enemies, that the people are not *divided* from their government.

There remains not the least doubt that their project of plundering this part of the globe, is very much strengthened by the fallacious idea that the Executive of the United States hath contravened the wishes and sentiments of the people at large, in his intercourse with foreign nations.

To

To repel this false and mischievous calumny as far as lies in our power, by bearing a public and unequivocal testimony in favor of your administration, and especially in behalf of the late attempt to negociate a treaty of peace with the French nation, is both our motive and apology for intruding on you with this address.

If our situation has become in any degree serious or alarming, we are highly gratified in the reflection it has not proceeded from any want of temperate and judicious measures, on your part, to prevent it.

The relative conduct of the United States and of France, at this eventful period, must form a striking contrast, in the judgment of the candid and discerning part of mankind; and history will hereafter be at a loss which to admire most, the impudent profligacy and exorbitant demands of the French, in order to plunge us into war, or the anxious and unremitted efforts of the United States to avoid it. While we thus express *our* unreserved approbation of the conduct of the first magistrate, we cannot omit the opportunity of declaring, that we have the most entire confidence in your wisdom, integrity, and political fortitude; and that we trust, by the blessings of Heaven, upon the executive and legislative councils of our country, aided by the patriotism of the people, we shall

ſhall be enabled to ſupport our independence, in defiance of an enemy, who not only ſpurns at our miniſters of peace, but openly avows an intention of compelling us to yield the laſt farthing; if, in their boundleſs ambition, they ſhall think proper to aſk it.

To the INHABITANTS *of* BERKS *County*.

GENTLEMEN,

THE public and unequivocal teſtimony you offer, in favor of my adminiſtration, eſpecially in the late attempt to negociate a treaty of peace with the French nation, deſerves my thanks.

I think with you, that hiſtory will hereafter be at a loſs which to admire moſt, the anxious and unremitted efforts of the United States to avoid war, or thoſe of the French to plunge us into it.

Your approbation and confidence are equally encouraging, and I truſt with you, that by the bleſſings of Heaven, on the legiſlative and executive councils of our country, ſupported by the patriotiſm of the people, we ſhall be enabled to preſerve our independence.

JOHN ADAMS.

To the PRESIDENT, *the* SENATE, *and House of* REPRESENTATIVES *of the* UNITED STATES.

AT a time when the ſituation of our country has become truly critical, the citizens of Montgomery county, feel it an incumbent duty to join in the general expreſſion of regret that the unreaſonable overbearance of a foreign nation ſhould mar the peaceful happineſs we enjoy under the beſt of governments, and that the honorable efforts which have been made uſe of to preſerve our peace, ſhould have failed of the wiſhed for ſucceſs.

Under ſuch circumſtances, permit us to expreſs our ſatisfaction and full confidence in the conſtituted authorities of our country, and our determination to ſupport them in the meaſures which they may find expedient to adopt for the preſervation of the peace, honor and independence of our country. Whatever political ſentiments we may, as individuals entertain, we truſt that on this head there will be but one voice, and that no previous predilections will, under any circumſtances, induce us directly or indirectly, to favor the enemies of our country, and of the happy conſtitution and government under which we live.

To

To the CITIZENS *of* MONTGOMERY *County*.

GENTLEMEN,

YOUR addreſs to the Preſident, Senate and Houſe of Repreſentatives, has been preſented to me by your committee.

The general expreſſions of regret that the unreaſonable overbearance of a foreign nation ſhould mar the peaceful happineſs we enjoy under the beſt of governments, are natural, but will not ſoften the hearts of our oppreſſors. It is not in mortals by the moſt honorable efforts, at all times to command ſucceſs or preſerve peace.

The ſatisfaction and full confidence you expreſs in the conſtituted authorities of your country, and your determination to ſupport them, in the meaſures which they may find expedient to adopt, for the preſervation of the peace, honor and independence of our country, are conſonant to the character of worthy citizens; and theſe ſentiments are rendered the more exemplary, for the reſervation you make of your political ſentiments as individuals, and your previous predilections.

JOHN ADAMS.

To *His Excellency* JOHN ADAMS, PRESIDENT *of the* UNITED STATES.

SIR,

THE day set apart by the President of the United States, to implore the mercy and benediction of Heaven on our country, the inhabitants of Huntingdon county, consider as a proper occasion to express to His Excellency the President their sentiments on the afflictive and hazardous situation in which the United States are placed.

The inhabitants of this county have considered with an attention its importance demanded, the conduct of this government towards the French republic. And in that review they discover the most sincere and ardent desire on the part of our government to preserve a most strict and honorable neutrality with the world, and to cultivate in an especial manner, peace and harmony with the French nation.

Your instructions to the commissioners to the French nation have evidenced a disposition to remove every cause of complaint, however groundless and frivolous, and to make sacrifices seldom equalled in the history of a people desirous of retaining their sovereignty and independence. These commissioners have not been received, these overtures would not be suffered to be made known,

known, and it is demanded of the American people, to become the tributaries of a foreign nation. The people of this country have been represented by our domestic enemies to our foreign ones, as divided from the government, as dissatisfied with the constitution, the President, and the administration, and as disposed to submit cheerfully, to any imposition the interest or ambition of France might require. For ourselves and our country, and we trust for our State, we pronounce this to be untrue.—Attached to our constitution, confiding in the President and those who administer the affairs of the United States, we now declare our most perfect reliance on our rulers, our most dedecided approbation of the measures of our public councils, and our determination to support these councils and measures at every risk.

Although we deprecate war as one of the greatest mischiefs, yet we consider submission to the insolent and degrading terms held out as the price of peace, to be one of the greatest indignities that can be offered to a nation, and only the wicked prelude to future insults and demands.

The inhabitants of this county assure you, Sir, that your accession to the Presidential chair, was the warmest wish of their hearts, and that your administration has been such

as

The voice of our fellow-citizens addressed to you from various parts of the United States, on this momentous occasion, affords us a pleasing consolation; while it evinces a degree of union and firmness that may preserve our country from further degradation.

Permit us to express our sincere regret, that every overture consistent with the dignity of our government, has been tried in vain for the amicable adjustment of our difference with France and for the attainment of peace. While we reflect, that the inhabitants of this place have not been exempted from the severest sufferings which war inflicts, we have reason to appreciate the blessings of peace; but we can never consent to purchase peace at the expense of our national honor and sovereignty. With these impressions, we do most solemnly pledge ourselves to the extent of our abilities and at the risk of our lives, to support such measures as have been, or may be adopted by the Executive of our government, to preserve inviolate our independence and national dignity, and to protect our civil and religious rights.

To the INHABITANTS *of* LUZERNE *County*.

GENTLEMEN,

I THANK you for this address, presented to me by your representative in Congress, Mr. Sitgreaves.

The

The arts and address, deception and seduction which have been employed for so many years to divide us, are likely to end in our more perfect union.

If *your* experience of the severest sufferings which war inflicts, cannot intimidate you to purchase peace at the expense of national honor and sovereignty, there is not another place in the United States which ought not to blush at the idea.

The solemn pledge of yourselves at the risk of your lives, and to the extent of your abilities to support the measures of government, to preserve inviolate our national dignity, must be confided in by all who know any thing of your history.

JOHN ADAMS.

From the Commissioned OFFICERS *of the* MILITIA, *the* TROOP *of* HORSE, *and the* CITIZENS *of* WESTMORELAND *County, to the* PRESIDENT *of the* UNITED STATES *of* AMERICA.

SIR,

WHEN the government and existence of the United States, as an independent nation, are threatened by a domineering foreign power, whose ambition, insolence and rapacity are almost unexampled in civilized

as they expected—*firm and dignified*, desirous of preserving the peace of this country, yet determined in your hands its honor should not be tarnished, its sovereignty diminished, or its independence destroyed.

To the INHABITANTS *of* HUNTINGDON *County.*

GENTLEMEN,

THE day you selected to express to me your sentiments, on the afflictive and hazardous situation in which the United States are placed, gives them a peculiar solemnity.

When, on that serious day, you declared you discovered in the conduct of government, after an attentive consideration, the most sincere and ardent desire to preserve a strict and honorable neutrality, and to cultivate, in an especial manner, peace and harmony with the French nation, the world will entertain no doubt of your sincerity.

Although, with you, I deprecate *war*, yet I cannot but think that there are many other mischiefs still greater—a depravation of general principle; submission to a restless, insidious, perfidious foreign influence; national dishonor and disgrace, are calamities more deplorable.

JOHN ADAMS.

From

From the Inhabitants *of* Luzerne *County, to the* President *of the* United States.

SIR,

WHILE we have the utmoſt confidence in the widom, integrity and abilities of thoſe who are conſtitutionally entruſted with the management of our national concerns, we conceive it would be improper to expreſs an opinion relative to the meaſures neceſſary to be taken at this important criſis in our public affairs: but viewing with indignation, the unprovoked, wanton and cruel attack made upon our national rights, by the arbitrary rulers of France, we ſhould deem ourſelves unworthy the bleſſings we enjoy under our free and happy government, ſhould we remain ſilent.

The repeated inſults offered our government, and the continued depredations committed on American property, by the French nation—the mean and degrading terms they hold out, as the only baſis on which they will negociate—and above all, their baſe inſinuations that the people of America are ſo abandoned that they will tamely ſubmit to, and even juſtify ſuch outrages on their property, and ſuch indignities to their government; are ſufficient to excite the abhorrence and awaken the energy of every true American.

The

times, it appears to be an important duty in the citizens to avow their detestation of the vile attempt.

The people of America at first viewed the cause of France with emotions of favorable regard; but the relative situation of their country, and the wish of cultivating peace with all mankind, coinciding with that state of neutrality which they owed to other allies and friendly powers in Europe, determined their Executive, at an early period of the contest, to adopt an impartial conduct, of which none could justly complain. That policy has uniformly met with the approbation of the legislature, and received the concurrence of all good and well informed citizens. This moderation on the part of the government, the supplies afforded by them to France and her colonies at critical periods, and the general approbation by the citizens, who on many occasions favored her cause, have, since the intoxication produced by conquest, been returned with depredations, injuries and insults, without the colour of right or rational excuse. It is no small satisfaction, however, to observe that all the perfidious machinations of the rulers in that country, to sow divisions among the people of this, and to induce distrust of their own administration, have only contributed to cement the union, and call forth the expression of that independent and manly spirit to

oppose

heir enemies, without which the liberty is but a delusive sound.

services, Sir, in the cause of your in spite of all that calumny could cast a veil over them, have placed he distinguished station you now Your experience has sufficiently ou that malice and injustice will ever eir rage against their opposite vir- t that Providence, ever just and , though his ways may not be tra- ly crowns with his blessing the pa- forts of those who steadily pursue c weal. That you, and all to whom tions of authority in these United committed, may be immoveable in uit, and that your labors may meet decided countenance and support ue Americans, to the confusion of n as well as private enemies, is the ope and desire of a general meeting mmissioned officers of the militia of eland county, of the troop of horse, numerous assemblage of citizens, sburgh, on the anniversary of the ence of the United States.

also beg leave to add the assurance espect for your official character, wishes for your individual welfare; s of their determination to oppose ies of their government and coun- ery shape.

To

To the Commissioned OFFICERS *of the* MILITIA, *the* TROOP *of* HORSE, *and the* CITIZENS *of* WESTMORELAND *County*.

GENTLEMEN,

I RECEIVE, with peculiar pleaſure, this addreſs from Weſtmoreland county, which has been preſented to me by Mr. Sitgreaves.

It is not ſurpriſing that the people of America, at firſt, viewed the cauſe of France with favorable regards; a conſiderable portion of Europe felt the ſame emotions, and awful indeed have been the calamities brought on ſeveral nations by the deception. Let us learn wiſdom by their misfortunes!

Our ſyſtem of neutrality was dictated by prudence, juſtice and humanity; it has been continued until we were forced out of it by ſuch treatment as never was before offered by one nation to another, and patiently borne.

The intoxication produced by conqueſt, was never more extravagant. It has opened the eyes of the diſſenters, the republicans, and even the oppoſition in England. It is a high ſatisfaction to obſerve, that all the perfidious machinations to ſow diviſions among the people of this country, and to induce a diſtruſt of their own adminiſtration, have contributed to cement the union,

and

and call forth the expreſſion of an independent and manly ſpirit.

The obliging manner in which you are pleaſed to take notice of my ſervices, demands my thanks; and I return your kind wiſhes for my individual welfare, with great ſincerity.

JOHN ADAMS.

To the PRESIDENT *of the* UNITED STATES.

SIR,

AT a time when the minds of men are ſo intoxicated with ideas of reform, and viſionary ſchemes for meliorating the condition of humanity, as to be fatally inattentive to their own ſecurity, and regardleſs of conſiderations which have hitherto been deemed the moſt ſacred and obligatory; there may be a propriety in the declaration of ſentiments, which, in more ſettled times, might at leaſt be thought ſuperfluous. From the generality alſo of the practice of expreſſing approbation of the meaſures of government, at the preſent criſis, motives might be attached to the omiſſion of it, leſs honorable than a diſinclination to intrude upon the managers of the public concerns, or a reluctance to ſuppoſe that, in the reſiſtance of outrage and maintenance of national independence, they would not receive the ſupport of the virtuous and unprejudiced part of the community.

Under these impressions, we, the subscribers, inhabitants of the borough of Harrisburgh, beg leave to declare, that we are too highly sensible of the prosperity we enjoy, to be willing to relinquish it without an effort for its preservation; and that, in our wishes for the happiness of others, we have not lost sight of our country and ourselves.—That, in our opinion, the conduct and designs of the French republic (scarcely aggravated or made more apparent by the profligacy of their avowal) are such as to produce alarm and indignation in every breast which feels for the honor and happiness of America, and to excite the apprehensions of every man, of whatever nation or country, who may place a sense of justice, morality, and piety, among the ornaments of his nature and the blessings of society—That, under this persuasion, we hold it wise to be prepared for every event, and shall therefore most cheerfully acquiesce in such measures of defence, as may be adopted by you, Sir, and the other branches of the administration, at the present momentous period. And as your past conduct has invariably commanded the respect and approbation of every ingenuous mind, so we have the most perfect reliance that, in future, it will continue to be influenced by the purest

motives

motives and clearest perceptions of the public good.

We beg you to accept our cordial wishes for your personal welfare and happiness.

To the INHABITANTS *of the Borough of* HARRISBURGH.

GENTLEMEN,

YOUR address has been presented to me by Mr. Hartley, Mr. Sitgreaves, and Mr. Hanna, three of your representatives in Congress.

I know not which to admire most, the conciseness, the energy, the elegance, or profound wisdom of this excellent address.

Ideas of reformation, and schemes for meliorating the condition of humanity, should not be discouraged, when proposed with reason and pursued with moderation; but the rage for innovation, which destroys every thing because it is established, and introduces absurdities, the most monstrous, merely because they are new; was never carried to such a pitch of madness in any age of the world, as in this latter end of the boasted eighteenth century, and never produced effects so horrible upon suffering humanity.

Among all the appearances, portentous of evil, there is none more incomprehensible than

than the professions of republicanism among those who place not a sense of justice, morality, or piety, among the ornaments of their nature and the blessings of society. As nothing is more certain and demonstrable than that free republicanism cannot exist without these ornaments and blessings, the tendency of the times is rapid towards a restoration of the petty military despotisms of the feudal anarchy, and by their means a return to the savage state of barbarous life.

How can the press prevent this, when all the presses of a nation, and indeed of many nations at once, are subject to an imprimatur, by a veto upon pain of conflagration, banishment, or confiscation?

That America may have the glory of arresting this torrent of error, vice and imposture, is my fervent wish; and if sentiments, as great as those from Harrisburgh, should be found universally to prevail, as I doubt not they will, my hopes will be as sanguine as my wishes.

JOHN ADAMS.

From the PEOPLE *of* POTT'S TOWN *and its vicinity, in* MONTGOMERY *County, to* JOHN ADAMS, PRESIDENT *of the* UNITED STATES.

SIR,

WE have been accuſtomed to obſerve in ſilence, though not with indifference, thoſe political occurrences which affect the happineſs and proſperity of our country. The preſent eventful criſis, however, imposes on us a new duty, and we comply with its obligation with cheerfulneſs in expreſſing to you, the firſt officer of our government, thoſe ſentiments with which we are at preſent actuated.

We aſſure you, therefore, that we have cordially approved of the firm, yet temperate ſyſtem adopted by the Executive in its intercourſe with the government of the French republic. With anxious ſolicitude we have awaited the event of theſe overtures dictated by a ſpirit of dignified forbearance, and conducted with the firmneſs of conſcious integrity, which have been made with a view to an amicable adjuſtment of the differences between the two countries.—But, Sir, though we deſired an adjuſtment upon terms compatible with the honor and dignity of the United States, upon thoſe terms only, we deſired it, and we have ſeen, with

with inexpressible indignation, the infamous attempts which have been made upon the integrity of our government, by threatening the peace and happiness of our country, unless preserved at the price of national degradation.

With the virtuous spirit, therefore, of republicans, we join, we trust, the general voice, in rejecting with disdain the ignominious alternative; resolved to preserve inviolate, at the sacrifice, if necessary, of property and life, the honor and independence of our country, and to leave them unsullied, a sacred deposit with our posterity.

While a review of the measures of your administration impresses us with a sense of your wisdom and firmness, it inspires us with a confidence that you will not surrender any of the rights of the nation, and that its interest and happiness will still continue the object of your meritorious exertions.

To the PEOPLE *of* POTT'S TOWN *and its vicinity, in the County of* MONTGOMERY.

GENTLEMEN,

WE live in times, when it is almost impossible to observe with indifference, or in silence, those political occurrences, which affect the happiness and prosperity of our country.

The

The cordial approbation and respect you avow of the firm and temperate system, adopted by the executive authority of government, in its intercourse with the government of the French republic, is very satisfactory: You desired an adjustment upon terms compatible with the honor and dignity of the United States, and upon these terms only: You have seen, with inexpressible indignation, the infamous attempts which have been made upon the integrity of our government, by threatening the peace and happiness of your country, unless preserved at the price of national degradation: You resolve to preserve inviolate, at the sacrifice of life and property, the honor and independence of your country, and to leave them unsullied, a sacred deposit with posterity: and in declaring these sentiments to the world, you have deserved well of your country.

Your confidence that I will not surrender the rights of the nation, shall not be betrayed: If the nation were capable of such a surrender, which it is not, some other hand must affix the signature to the ignominious deed.

JOHN ADAMS.

To

To the PRESIDENT *of the* UNITED STATES.

SIR,

WE the ſubſcribers being a joint committee on the part of reſpectable meetings of the inhabitants of the towns of Sunbury and Northumberland, and the vicinities thereof, holden for the purpoſe of expreſſing their ſentiments of the meaſures purſued by our government, with reſpect to France, and to declare to you their unanimous determination to ſupport all the conſtituted authorities of the United States; beg leave to obſerve, that although among the laſt to addreſs you at this important era of our national independence, yet not the leaſt affectionate. Uninfluenced and almoſt unacquainted with the common forms uſed on occaſions of this kind, we ſhall ſpeak the language of our hearts, in the ſtyle of a free people to their firſt magiſtrate, and aſſure you, that it is with admiration and pleaſure we have beheld your conduct ſince called to the important office you now fill, evidencing the ſtrongeſt attachment to the intereſt of your fellow-citizens, by reſiſting with a firmneſs and dignity becoming the father of freemen, the intrigues of an artful and perfidious nation, tending as we conceive, not only to involve us in war, but to the deſtruction of that government whoſe ſalutary regulations we experience as daily bleſſings.

We

We cannot but lament as men, and as citizens, that a nation, once the friend and ally of America, once her supporter in the hour of danger, should be so changed and fallen; at a time when she declared to the world that her object was to establish a free government, she had our warmest wishes for success; but we view her now as a nation whose predominant passion is power; trampling on all those principles which assimilate man to his Maker, boldly attempting to colonize the world and render every part of it subservient to her views! We see her in fact as a Mount Ætna, casting from her, principles which have a tendency to consume religion, virtue and liberty. Her treatment to this country, we conceive is unparalleled in the history of civilized nations; she has wantonly committed depredations on our commerce, and almost destroyed our trade, without cause, and without provocation; her complaints of the treaty, made between Great Britain and this country, we consider as the wicked pretence for plunder and piracy.

When we reflect on the wisdom, mildness, and prudence which have marked every step taken by you, as the head of our government, to effect an amicable adjustment of all differences, and to obtain a recompense for the injuries our fellow-citizens have sustained, our hearts glow with love and affection for you, while they burn with indignation at the treatment received from the French government:—It is with pleasure that we assure you that the publication of your instructions to our envoys, and their dispatches, have been attended with the happiest effects; all the respectable yeomanry of our country are now united in the support of our government and its measures. We tender our services and purses to our government, to support it in any system of defence it may think proper to adopt. We are attached to peace, but it is the peace of freemen, and we shudder at the idea of sacrificing our independence for the permission of any nation on earth, to remain in quietude on our farms.

Our sincerest wishes for your health, and happiness, attend you; and we pray the great Disposer of human events to continue to bless and endow you with wisdom and fortitude to govern us, in this hour of difficulty.

To the INHABITANTS *of the Towns of* SUNBURY *and* NORTHUMBERLAND, *and their vicinity:*

GENTLEMEN,

I HAVE received from the hand of Colonel Hubley, your address, by your committee.

When

When you observe, that, although among the last to address me, at this important crisis, you are not the least affectionate; when you assure me it is with pleasure you have beheld my conduct, since called to the important office I now hold, evidencing the strongest attachment to the interest of my fellow-citizens, becoming the father of freedom; when you assure me, that your hearts glow with love and affection for me, while they burn with indignation at the treatment received, from the French government,—you touch the tender sensibilities of my heart, and excite my warmest gratitude.

I wish it were in my power to soften the colours of your picture of those who injure and insult us.

JOHN ADAMS.

To JOHN ADAMS, President *of the* United States *of* America.

SIR;

ON the birth-day of the United States, and at an era the most interesting that has occurred since their existence as a nation, the Pennsylvania State Society of the Cincinnati desire most respectfully to congratulate and address you.

As a portion of that band, whose best efforts were employed to establish the sovereignty

eignty and independence of our country, we come, in the moment of impending hostility, to offer the remnant of our lives to defend them.

The rights and privileges of America were not purchased with the best blood of her citizens, to be ingloriously surrendered on the requisition of a foreign power.

No, Sir, the spirit which procured, survives to protect them—And we rejoice to behold that spirit pre-eminently displayed in the firm, virtuous and dignified conduct of the federal chief magistrate. Our citizens of all ages are emulous of this illustrious example; the exertions of our youth declare that they have not degenerated, and afford an unquestionable assurance that their noble inheritance will be preserved unimpaired, and transmitted inviolate to posterity.

The government of France, abandoning every principle on which their revolution was predicated, has exhibited a spirit of despotism unexampled in the history of nations.

After perpetrating the most unprovoked and unjustifiable wrongs against the people of the United States, their rulers have rejected the reiterated advances of our government towards an explanation of differences; they have spurned our messengers of peace; and they have superadded insult to injury, in the exaction of an ignominious tribute.

tribute, which they hoped to extort by base intrigue, or to enforce by imperious menace.

As Americans, and as men, having a common interest in the welfare of the world, we rejoice that these outrages against its happiness have been resisted.

To the prudence, moderation and liberality of those measures of your administration, Sir, which we are convinced were sincerely directed to the attainment of an honorable peace, we render the approbation of citizens who justly appreciate that desirable position. To your vigilance and virtue, which have detected and repelled the attempts of avarice and ambition, on the part of the French government, against the United States, we offer the tribute of an higher applause. We desire to express the esteem and gratitude of citizens, who hold every consideration as secondary to the sovereignty and independence of our country—for the maintenance of which, and in support of every measure of our government that may be deemed necessary to protect the persons, privileges and property of our citizens, we do hereby pledge to you the solemn assurance of our utmost exertions.

To the PENNSYLVANIA STATE SOCIETY of the CINCINNATI.

GENTLEMEN,

THIS reſpectful addreſs, from gentlemen of your long experience, high rank, and authority in ſociety, and eminent ſervices to the nation, does me great honor.

"On the return of this auſpicious anniverſary at an era the moſt intereſting, I beg leave to reciprocate your kind congratulations—the fundamental and immutable principles of your ſociety, requiring an inceſſant attention to preſerve inviolate thoſe rights and liberties of human nature, for which you have fought and bled, and an unalterable determination to promote and cheriſh between the reſpective States that union and national honor ſo eſſentially neceſſary to their happineſs, and the dignity of the American republic, were never more indiſpenſable in all claſſes of citizens, or becoming your characters, than at this time—as a portion of that band, whoſe efforts were employed to eſtabliſh the ſovereignty of the United States, you, who have enjoyed the work of your own arms, and the fruits of a righteous and glorious war, muſt have viewed with inexpreſſible pleaſure, the increaſing proſperity and greatneſs of your country. You muſt now ſee, your tranquillity diſturbed, and your independence threatened, with indignation

dignation and contempt—the spirit which first asserted the sovereignty of this country, survives to maintain it, and your acknowledgment of some remaining portion of that spirit in the federal chief magistrate, is very honorable to him.

As it is but too manifest that unlawful depredations on our commerce will be continued, as long as it shall remain unprotected, so it is equally clear that all hopes of accommodation are at an end, until you and your associates throughout the Union, at the head of the rising generation, who are worthy to succeed you, shall have drawn your swords, once more in the cause of your country, and defended its just rights and sovereignty by your utmost exertions.

I pray you to accept of my best wishes for your health and long life, and that your latter days may be crowned with laurels, as unfading as the former.

JOHN ADAMS.

To the PRESIDENT *of the* UNITED STATES.

SIR,

THE students of Dickinson College, assembled again after the usual vacation, embrace the earliest opportunity of making a public and explicit declaration of their sentiments

l resolutions at this important

; that unanimity is of infinite im- the citizens, of these States, and ost unequivocal proofs of such hould be now given by the citi- e; we, the pupils of a seminary, are taught highly to prize our ment and all the blessings of lib- v, feel it our indispensable duty ir mite into the treasury of pub- ts.

be supposed that youths of our n be deeply versed in political ;—yet we know what *liberty* can in some measure estimate ice of *national dignity* and *inde-* ind we cannot be ignorant of are known to all the world.

ensible that we live under one of e and happy governments that isted; and we also know, that oted, under the smiles of Heav- rtue and patriotism of our fath- blessings we enjoy. We trust rit their spirit, and shall always noble example.

in the wisdom and integrity of and trusting that their aim has preserve this country from any in the convulsions of Europe,

we

we join with our fellow-citizens in approving and applauding the measures that have been pursued to maintain a state of neutrality and peace.

But what do we hear,—proclaimed by the highest authority?—That a nation, whom we were taught from our earliest years to call our friends, intoxicated with their victories, and apparently grasping at universal empire, says, 'We shall no longer be a neutral power; that we must retract our complaints of their hostile measures and become in fact their tributaries, before they will admit our envoys to an audience.' Such language and demands cannot fail to rouse the indignant spirit of Americans, and create an indissoluble union of all, both old and young, in the common cause. The yielding of a single point, in obedience to unjust and imperious requisitions, would, in our opinion, be to surrender our independence:—for a tame submission to one insult would only invite a repetition; till we should at length become a most degraded people, and our name, as a nation, be blotted from the records of time.

While such terms of peace and reconciliation are urged by the minister of France, the organ of the Directory, as appear to our government to be inadmissible, and the depredations on our commerce still continue and

and increase, we conceive that to neglect the means of self-defence, would be highly criminal, and evidence a most abject spirit. If there be any among us who would still plead the cause of France, and attempt to paralyse the efforts of our government, they ought to be esteemed our greatest enemies.

For our part, we reject with abhorrence every idea of submission to the will of a foreign power, and shall cheerfully leave the pleasing walks of science, when the voice of our country calls, to repel every attack upon our rights, liberty and independence.

To you, Sir, we look up with confidence, as the patron of science, liberty and religion; rejoicing to find that in every thing which flows from your pen, you consider these as the choicest blessings of humanity, which have an inseparable union, and without whose joint influence no society can be great, flourishing and happy.

While we ardently pray that the American republic may always rise superior to her enemies, and transmit the pure principles of liberty to the latest ages, we join at the same time, with the millions of America, in beseeching Heaven to bestow its choicest blessings on our beloved President.

To

To the STUDENTS *of* DICKINSON COLLEGE.

GENTLEMEN,

I HAVE received from the hand of one of your senators in Congress, Mr. Bingham, your public and explicit declaration of your sentiments and resolutions, at this important crisis, in an excellent address.

Although it ought not to be supposed, that young gentlemen of your standing should be deeply versed in political disquisitions, because your time has been occupied in the pursuit of the elements of science and literature in general, yet the feelings of nature are a sure guide in circumstances like the present. I need not, however, make this apology for you; few addresses, if any, have appeared, more correct in principle, better arranged and digested, more decent and moderate, better reasoned and supported, or more full, explicit and determined.

Since the date of your address, a fresh instance of the present spirit of a nation, or its government, whom you have been taught to call your friends, has been made public: two of your envoys have been ordered out of the republic----Why? answer this for yourselves my young friends. A third has been permitted or compelled to remain----Why? to treat of loans, as preliminary to an audience, as the French government understands it--- to wait for further orders, as your

your envoy conceives. Has any ſovereign of Europe ever dictated to your country the perſon ſhe ſhould ſend as ambaſſador? Did the monarchy of France, or any other country, ever aſſume ſuch a dictatorial power over the ſovereignty of your country? Is the republic of the United States of America, a fief of the republic of France? It is a queſtion, whether even an equitable treaty, under ſuch circumſtances of indecency, inſolence and tyranny, ought ever to be ratified by an independent nation—there is however, no probability of any treaty, to bring this queſtion to a deciſion.

If there are any who ſtill plead the cauſe of France, and attempt to paralyſe the efforts of your government, I agree with you, they ought to be eſteemed our greateſt enemies. I hope that none of you, but ſuch as feel a natural genius and diſpoſition to martial exerciſe and exertions, will ever be called from the pleaſing walks of ſcience, to repel any attack upon your rights, liberties and independence.

When you look up to me, with confidence, as the patron of ſcience, liberty and religion, you melt my heart. Theſe are the choiceſt bleſſings of humanity—they have an inſeparable union; without their joint influence, no ſociety can be great, flouriſhing or happy.

While

While I ardently pray that the American republic may always rise superior to her enemies, and transmit the purest principles of liberty to the latest ages, I beseech Heaven to bestow its choicest blessings on the governors and students of your college, and all other seminaries of learning in America.

JOHN ADAMS.

DELAWARE.

To the PRESIDENT *of the* UNITED STATES.

SIR,

A NUMBER of the Officers of the Militia of Newcastle county, in the State of Delaware, impressed with the importance of the present crisis of public affairs, to the happiness and independence of the United States; and conceiving that the unjust and imperious conduct of the republic of France toward America, has been dictated in a great measure by the unfounded misrepresentations of her own agents, and some misguided and deluded citizens of this country, that the people and the government were divided and opposed to each other; we feel ourselves constrained by every consideration of duty to the constituted authorities, to ourselves, and to our country, to repel the insinuation which thus attempts to dishonor the American character.

Appreciating with due estimation, the advantages of neutrality and the blessings of peace, we have beheld with pleasure and entire satisfaction your earnest and repeated endeavors, and those of your predecessor, to preserve this desirable position; and we have seen with equal regret, that the anxious advances of our government to a restoration of harmony with the French republic, have been received with contemptuous disregard on their part; and at the moment when negociation ought to have produced redress, aggression has been increased, and further depredations authorized, under the vain hope of inducing a compliance with the wretched demands of avarice and corruption.

Little does France understand the American character in supposing we are to be frightened into mean compliances, by holding up to our view her dependent allies, a degraded Genoa, or a dismembered Venice. The picture raises just indignation in the minds of freemen, and will stimulate their exertions to avoid a similar fate.

With pain do we discover in the infancy of the French government, pretending to be a free republic, and founded upon the rights of man, the evidence of an active corruption

ruption that would degrade the most profligate tyranny—Fortunate for America! the ocean separates her from this seat of contagion, whose influence is destructive of all morals—and long may she enjoy under your prudent and wise administration, that happiness and prosperity which is the reward of public virtue and integrity.

Be assured, Sir, of our grateful approbation of the conduct heretofore pursued by you, to preserve peace and friendship with foreign powers; and our confidence in the wisdom and patriotism of every branch of the government; and we pledge ourselves as citizens and soldiers, firmly to support those measures which may hereafter be thought necessary to secure the constitution, freedom and independence of the United States.

To the OFFICERS *of the* MILITIA *of* NEW-CASTLE *County*.

GENTLEMEN,

YOUR address, which has been presented to me, in your behalf, by your senators and representatives in Congress, expresses sentiments and resolutions, well becoming the characters of Officers of the Militia, the object of whose institution is, the maintenance and security of the constitution, freedom and independence of their country.

The

The unjuſt and imperious conduct of a majority of the French Directory toward America, may have been dictated by miſrepreſentations of their own agents, and of deluded Americans; but there is too much reaſon to believe that an unbounded ambition for univerſal empire, and an inſatiable avarice of money, united with the delirium of victory, and a ſanguine confidence that they are, at leaſt for a time, the maſters of the world, have dictated their inſufferable arrogance, trampling alike on their own conſtitution, and the rights of their people; on the law of nations, and the faith of treaties.

It is indeed an awful conſideration, that at a time when a great part of Europe appears diſpoſed to adopt republican governments, a corruption ſhould appear, which never was exhibited before, by the moſt abſolute monarchies, or completeſt deſpotiſms.

It ſhould ſeem that fraud and force, were to be the only meaſure of right and wrong: —This ſyſtem muſt ſoon be changed, or ſcience, arts, virtue, liberty and peace, muſt be baniſhed, and a ſavage barbarity ſubſtituted in their places.

America is of too much importance to the world, for the purpoſes of wealth and power, to leave her the ſmalleſt hope of eſcaping, without her own determined exertions, the contagion of the general diſtemper.

Your

Your approbation and kind wishes are received with gratitude, and returned with sincerity.

JOHN ADAMS.

To the PRESIDENT of the UNITED STATES.

SIR,

WITH a solicitude equal to the important and interesting crisis which at this time agitates the public mind, added to a most sincere desire to convince the world, that no domestic divisions, or foreign machinations, aimed at the independence of our country, or intended to commit its honor, can ever succeed; we, the inhabitants of Kent county, in the State of Delaware, convened at Dover, beg leave to convey to you our most sincere and entire approbation of the wise, firm and conciliatory measures you have pursued to secure the blessings of peace, and to preserve unsullied and undiminished the safety, honor and independence of the United States.

As the constitutional organ of the United States, to settle and adjust differences with foreign nations, we feel no hesitation in declaring what we firmly believe, that you have done every thing to restore harmony, and continue the tranquillity of our country, that wisdom, policy and patriotism could possibly effect.

Under this view of your adminiſtration, much as we deprecate the calamities of war, yet when national diſgrace and a tame ſubmiſſion to the moſt immeaſurable inſults and aggreſſions on the part of the French republic, become the only alternative, we can ſafely offer you our moſt unqualified aſſurances,—that as Americans who underſtand the bleſſings of liberty and a good government, we ſhall never heſitate a moment in our choice. To avert theſe evils, we are ſorry to find that the moſt ſalutary meaſures which wiſdom and ſincerity could preſcribe, have not only been fruſtrated and diſregarded, but inſultingly repelled and defeated by the baſeſt attempts to extort from our country, even without a proſpect of retribution, immenſe ſums of money.

In every event, Sir, convinced of your wiſdom, energy and patriotiſm, we not only engage our utmoſt ſupport in the meaſures which government may ultimately adopt; but in caſe of an unavoidable appeal to arms, we pledge ourſelves to ſtand in conſtant readineſs, firmly to oppoſe, at all hazards, every enemy, whom either a miſtaken policy, luſt of dominion, or love of plunder, may induce to violate our rights, or in any manner to invade the peace, liberty or independence of our country.

That the Ruler of the univerſe may guide and protect the councils and government of

the

the United States, and long preserve your valuable life, is the sincere prayer of our hearts.

To the CITIZENS *of* KENT *County.*

GENTLEMEN,

YOUR resolutions and address unanimously adopted at Dover, have been presented to me by one of your senators in Congress, Mr. Latimer, and by your representative, Mr. Bayard.

I thank you for your sincere and entire approbation of the measures pursued to secure the blessings of peace, and to preserve unsullied and undiminished the safety, honor and independence of the United States.

Americans who know that the blessings of liberty, and a good government can never be enjoyed under national disgrace, and a tame submission to the most immeasurable insults and aggressions, can never hesitate a moment in their choice of measures.

When you engage your utmost support, to the measures which government may ultimately adopt, against the mistaken policy, lust of dominion, or love of plunder, which may violate our rights, or invade the peace, liberty and independence of our country, you give every assurance which the government can desire.

That

That supreme wisdom may guide, and Divine power protect the councils and arms of the United States, and long preserve and prosper the citizens of Kent, is the prayer of

JOHN ADAMS.

To JOHN ADAMS, PRESIDENT *of the* UNITED STATES *of* AMERICA.

SIR,

CONVINCED of your solicitude for the honor, independence and happiness of the United States, and of the justice of your administration toward foreign nations, the Grand Jury of the county of Sussex, in the State of Delaware, at this important crisis deem it a duty, to assure you of their perfect confidence in the wisdom and moderation of your councils, and of their entire approbation of the honest zeal you have displayed, to accommodate the differences between this country and the republic of France. And they doubt not that the same patriotic principles which have actuated you to persevere in your endeavors to preserve an honorable peace to your country, will, when the occasion shall require, animate you to defend with firmness and vigor those rights, of which, the constitution and laws have made you the guardian.

They

They pray God that these States may be still favored with his greatest blessing; but should all your attempts prove ineffectual, they trust they will not be wanting in yielding every possible support to their country in the hour of danger.

However they may heretofore have differed in mere speculative opinions, yet, Sir, they are unanimous in declaring their fixed determination to support an administration which has given entire satisfaction, and which they verily believe possesses the esteem and respect of the great body of the people.

To the GRAND JURY *of the County of* SUSSEX.

GENTLEMEN,

YOUR handsome address, which has been presented to me, demonstrates your attachment to your country, and is a sensible gratification to me.

If, as you believe, my administration has given entire satisfaction, one of the most ardent wishes of my heart will be satisfied, and as your obliging assurance of it is the highest reward in your power to bestow upon me, it receives my entire thanks.

JOHN ADAMS.

MARY-

MARYLAND.

The ADDRESS *and* MEMORIAL *of the* CITIZENS *of* BALTIMORE, *and* BALTIMORE *County, to the* PRESIDENT, *the* SENATE, *and the House of* REPRESENTATIVES *of the* UNITED STATES,—

RESPECTFULLY SHEWETH,

THAT your memorialists at this important and eventful crisis, when a foreign nation equally regardless of the faith of treaties and the law of nations, has menaced with destruction the freedom and independence of the United States, and represented the citizens thereof to be a divided people, feel themselves impelled by considerations of duty and love to their country, to express their sentiments and declare their determination to support the constituted authorities.

Your memorialists highly applaud the wise and liberal measures pursued by the government of the United States, for the adjustment of all differences, and restoration of harmony between this country and the French republic; measures, which, in their opinion, had for their object the preservation of peace, the faith of treaties, and the welfare of the United States. It is with regret we learn, that these advances to peace have

have been wantonly rejected, and our envoys not only denied an audience, but treated with the most marked contempt. A conduct like this, fails not to excite a spirit of indignation; and although warmly attached to peace and its consequent blessings, we cannot for a moment hesitate in making our election between freedom and servile submission to a foreign power.

Having the fullest confidence in the wisdom of our government, we submit to their consideration the necessity of placing our country in a state of defence, and protecting our commerce; and trust that in the adoption of such measures as sound policy may dictate, the consideration of expense and temporary inconvenience, resulting from the interruption of peace, will not be considered of such magnitude, as to be placed in competition with the sovereignty and freedom of the United States, whose existence is so unjustly threatened.

To the CITIZENS *of* BALTIMORE *and* BALTIMORE *County.*

GENTLEMEN,

I THANK you for communicating to me this respectful address.

The sense you entertain of the conduct of a foreign nation, in threatening with destruction,

ſtruction, the freedom and independence of the United States, and repreſenting the citizens of America as a divided people, is ſuch as patriotiſm, naturally and neceſſarily inſpires---The fate of every republic in Europe however, from Poland to Geneva, has given too much cauſe for ſuch thoughts and projects in our enemies, and ſuch apprehenſions in our friends and ourſelves.

Republics are always divided in opinions concerning forms of governments, and plans and details of adminiſtration---theſe diviſions are generally harmleſs, often ſalutary and ſeldom very hurtful, except when foreign nations interfere, and by their arts and agents excite and ferment them into parties and factions: ſuch interference and influence muſt be reſiſted and exterminated, or it will end in America, as it did anciently in Greece, and in our own time in Europe, in our total deſtruction, as a republican government, and independent power.

The liberal applauſe you beſtow on the meaſures purſued by the government, for the adjuſtment of differences, and reſtoration of harmony, your reſolutions of reſiſtance in preference to ſubmiſſion to any foreign power; your confidence in the government, your recommendation of meaſures of defence of the country and protection of its commerce, and your generous reſolu-

tion

tion to submit to the expenses and temporary inconveniencies which may be necessary to preserve the sovereignty and freedom of the United States, are received with much respect.

JOHN ADAMS.

From the GRAND LODGE *of* FREE MASONS, *to His Excellency* JOHN ADAMS, PRESIDENT *of the* UNITED STATES.

SIR,

ALTHOUGH it is a maxim of the Masonic fraternity, and which is most religiously adhered to, never to interfere in political subjects; yet if there ever was a season which could justify a deviation from this maxim, the present is that season; and we should deem ourselves culpable, at this moment, when the dangers of war threaten our country; at this moment, when the virulent and mercenary voice of party is employed to represent our institution as inimical to the security, not only of regular government, but even of Divine religion; did we not step forward publickly and explicitly to declare our sentiments of public measures, and our determination to support with our lives those sentiments in the issue.

"In the State, a Mason is to behave as a peaceable and dutiful subject."—This, Sir, is our great and only political principle; and among the first lessons which are taught on our entrance into a Masonic Lodge, is, submission to the laws and constituted authorities of the country in which we reside. ---He is no longer considered as a brother, who, in his character of a Mason, connives at the subversion of either.

With such a principle, and under such a government as ours, what must be our sentiments when we see that government and its representatives treated with a series of the most degrading and insupportable insults which the overgrown pride of a foreign nation can multiply upon it and them? Taught to estimate men and things by the noble and unvarying standard of impartial justice, what must be our feelings when we behold the property of our fellow-citizens seized and confiscated by the lawless hand of a predatory power, disdaining any other pretext than that which arms furnish for its justification? When we thus witness every right of neutrality and commerce violated, and the wide extent of ocean converted into a mart for piracy and plunder, aggravated by circumstances of the most unparalleled atrocity; when we sum up the immense catalogue of injuries which we have sustained from the French nation; what our sensations must be, we leave you, Sir, to judge. Language is inadequate to define them! To

your

your own breaſt we appeal: there you will find our ſentiments deeply written, in the characters of patriotiſm, fidelity and honor.

Strongly inclined, from the tenets of our fraternal inſtitution, to peace and good underſtanding with all the world, we deprecated war ſo long as we had any hope of its being poſſible to avoid it, conſiſtently with the reſpect due to our own national character. We have ſeen, we admire and applaud the honorable and dignified means which you have unceaſingly, though unſucceſsfully purſued, to render this hope productive; but we now fear it is no longer to be indulged, and are prepared for the worſt that may enſue.

As citizens, we love, reverence, and will, to the extent of the means we are capable of employing, ſupport the conſtitution which ſecures the liberty of our country. To do ſo is a duty---is a virtue; and the object of maſonry is, to confirm, not to deſtroy, a virtuous principle---to encourage its votaries in the practice of the ſocial as well as the moral duties, not to render them refractory to either. Maſonry, therefore, teaches us to love our country. And though we may view war as full of horrors, yet an age of warfare does not appear ſo horrid as one moment of peace, purchaſed by the ſurrender of independence. We only wait the ſignal.---

ſignal.—The ſtandard of our nation once unfurled, our lives, with thoſe of our fellow-citizens, ſhall form a barrier to defend it.

Permit us to offer you our moſt ſincere congratulations on an occaſion the moſt intereſting to Americans. We again behold our WASHINGTON ! the glory of his country---the boaſt, the honor of our ſociety and of mankind—relinquiſhing, in old age, the tranquil ſcene ! Summoned by the voice of his country, we again behold the hero and the patriot willing and forward to ſacrifice his private eaſe for her ſafety ! What heart can be ſo cold—what heart can ſo languidly move, as not to beat high and ſtrong at the thought of being once more commanded by that brighteſt ornament of the human character, our true, our beloved brother, GEORGE WASHINGTON !—The name alone will form a ſure defence !

Accept, Sir, our grateful thanks for thoſe patriotic exertions in ſupport of the independence and the honor of our nation, which we have uniformly witneſſed from you ; while we breathe to Heaven the fervent prayer, that the immortal Architect of the univerſe, the great Diſpenſer of the fate of nations, may long enable you to continue them.

To

To the FREE MASONS *of the State of* MARYLAND.

GENTLEMEN,

I THANK you for this generous and noble addrefs.

The zeal you difplay to vindicate your fociety from the imputations and fufpicions of being "inimical to regular government and Divine religion," is greatly to your honor. It has been an opinion of many confiderate men, as long as I can remember, that your fociety might, in fome time or other, be made an inftrument of danger and diforder to the world. Its ancient exiftence, and univerfal prevalence, are good proofs that it has not heretofore been applied to mifchievous purpofes; and in this country, I prefume that no one has *attempted* to employ it for purpofes foreign from its *original* inftitution. But in an age, and in countries, where *morality* is, by fuch numbers, confidered as mere *convenience*, and *religion* a *lie*, you are better judges than I am, whether ill ufes have been or may be made of Mafonry.

Your appeal to my own breaft, and your declaration that I fhall *there* find your fentiments, I confider as a high compliment; and feel a pride in perceiving and declaring, that the opinions, principles and feelings expreffed, are conformable to my own.

With you, I fear that no hope remains, but in preparation for the worst that may ensue.

Persevere, gentlemen, in revering the constitution which secures your liberties; in loving your country; in practising the *social*, as well as the *moral* duties; in presenting your lives, with those of your fellow-citizens, a barrier to defend your independence. And may the Architect all-powerful surround you with walls impregnable, and receive you, finally, (your country happy, prosperous and glorious!) to mansions eternal in the Heavens.

With heart-felt satisfaction, I reciprocate your most sincere congratulations on an occasion the most interesting to Americans: no light or trivial cause would have given you the opportunity of beholding your WASHINGTON again relinquishing the tranquil scene, in delicious shades. To complete the character of French philosophy, and French policy, at the end of the eighteenth century, it seemed to be necessary to combat this patriot and hero.

JOHN ADAMS.

RESOLUTIONS *adopted unanimously, by the* CITIZENS *of* CALVERT *County.*

I. THAT the President of the United States is entitled to the thanks of this meeting,

ing, for his prudent, firm and patriotic administration, and for his wise, candid and sincere endeavors to obtain an amicable adjustment of the unhappy dispute with the French republic.

II. That our envoys, in the discharge of their duty, merit our esteem and approbation.

III. That although we sincerely deprecate a war (with all its concomitant calamities) with any foreign power, yet we will most cheerfully encounter every danger, rather than submit to the depredations so dishonorably committed on our commerce.

IV. That we view with abhorrence the attempts made by foreigners and others, to alienate our fellow-citizens from the government of their choice, that we are determined to support the constituted authorities of the United States, and that we will repel any invasion on our rights and liberties, at the risk of every thing that is dear and valuable.

V. That the chairman be requested to enclose the foregoing resolutions to the representative of this district, to be by him presented to the President and Congress of the United States.

To the CITIZENS *of* CALVERT *County.*

GENTLEMEN,

YOUR resolutions have been communicated to me, according to your desire, by your representative in Congress, Mr. Dent.

Your thanks unanimously voted to me, are a great reward, and your esteem and approbation of our envoys in the discharge of their duty, is very acceptable to me.

Your resolutions most cheerfully to encounter every danger, rather than to submit to the depredations on our commerce, so dishonorably committed, and the abhorrence with which you view the attempts made by foreigners and others to alienate our fellow-citizens from the government of their choice, your determination to support the constituted authorities of the United States, and repel every invasion of your rights and liberties, at the risk of every thing that is dear and valuable, are wise and virtuous.

JOHN ADAMS.

To the PRESIDENT *of the* UNITED STATES.

SIR,

AT this eventful period, when the dignity and independence of the United States are involved; at a time when a foreign nation has

has declared (among other enormous requisites) that money to an immense amount must be paid as a preliminary to an audience with the Directory, or their recognition of our envoys extraordinary to that nation; and at a time when a foreign nation attempts to degrade the American character, by declaring to the world, that they have in the bosom of our country a considerable party attached to their interests, or devoted to their mandates, with a view to overawe our councils; that the fate of Venice is held out to us as a punishment in reserve for our country; that their ships of war should ravage and plunder our sea-coasts, should their demands not be complied with—This painful picture, sent to us by our commissioners, in whom we repose full confidence, from a government so congenial to our own, from a nation to whom our best wishes extended in their arduous struggles for independence, is a strange and wonderful spectacle of man!—We, the subscribers, inhabitants of Washington county, and State of Maryland, anxious for peace with all the world, and being possessed of full information of your conduct with respect to France, have no doubt, Sir, but that you, with the other branches of our government, will yet meet, with sincerity, every honorable overture of that nation, for the final adjustment of the differences unhappily subsisting between

tween us; fully impressed with those ideas, we have only to declare that your conduct with respect to France, has been fair, ample and honorable, and receives our most hearty approbation, and having then the utmost confidence in the integrity and wisdom of our national government, we are resolved, at the risk of our lives and property, to support it, as one of our own choice, and the hard earned independence of our country.

To the INHABITANTS *of* WASHINGTON *County.*

GENTLEMEN,

YOUR address has been presented to me by your representative in Congress, Mr. Baer.

When you say that the government of France is congenial to your own, I pray you, gentlemen, to reconsider the subject. The constitution, the administration, the laws, and their interpretation in France, are as essentially different from ours, as the ancient monarchy. If we may believe travellers returned from that country, or their own committees, the pomp and magnificence, the profusion of expense, the proud usurpation, the domineering inequality at present in that country, as well as the prostitution of morals and depravation of manners, exceed all that ever was seen under

the

the old monarchy, and form the most perfect contrast to your own in all those respects. —I shall meet, with sincerity, any honorable overtures of that nation, but I shall make no more overtures.

JOHN ADAMS.

To the PRESIDENT *of the* UNITED STATES.

SIR,

WE, the subscribers, being a committee on the part of a respectable meeting of the citizens of Worcester county, in the State of Maryland, convened at Snowhill for the purpose of expressing their sense of the conduct of our government in regard to its foreign relations, and to declare their determination at this pressing crisis to support it, do communicate to you as the unanimous sense of the said meeting, that your attempts to restore that harmony between the United States and the French republic, which has been so unfortunately impaired, and to reinstate that good understanding between the two nations so desirable to the lovers of peace, have been wise and prudent, and entitle you to the highest evidence of their esteem. Impressed as they are with the wisdom and propriety of the measures hitherto pursued in the administration of our government, sensible of our present alarming situation,

tion, and believing that our difficulties have been occasioned in a great measure by internal and foreign machinations, calculated to produce in France an unfounded opinion that the Americans are a divided people: In order to aid in removing an opinion so injurious to our national character and so hazardous to our peace, they will never hesitate to proclaim to the world their determination, and they do hereby pledge themselves to you, to support any measures which may be adopted by the government of their country calculated to support their rights and assert the dignity of the nation. Whilst we thus express to you the approbation and determination of our fellow-citizens, we cannot forbear to declare our abhorrence of the profligate and disgraceful conduct of the government of France, which has been disclosed in the dispatches from our envoys. While we lament the unfortunate necessity of having to negociate with characters who do not hesitate to acknowledge their own prostitution, and to declare that the justice of our claims will avail us nothing; but that the only measure of their exactions is the extent of their power—To this conduct, those amiable principles of religion, morality and forbearance, contained in your late proclamation, exhibit to Americans a pleasing contrast.

Permit

Permit us alſo to indulge a hope, that in this threatening proſpect of our affairs, harmony and unanimity may pervade our public councils and our citizens at large, and to expreſs our unfeigned wiſhes for your health and happineſs in the trying ſituation in which you are placed.

To the COMMITTEE *of a Meeting of* CITIZENS *of* WORCESTER *County.*

GENTLEMEN,

I HAVE received, from the hands of your repreſentative, Mr. Dennis, your letter, expreſſing the ſenſe of the citizens aſſembled at Snowhill.

Your approbation of the meaſures of government, and determination to ſupport them, are very acceptable.

The diſpatches exhibit a ſcene of corruption, depravity and intrigue, which is diſgraceful to human nature—a ſtriking contraſt to the conduct of our envoys:—I am happy to find you obſerve in it a contraſt to thoſe amiable principles of religion, morality and forbearance, contained in a late Proclamation. Every lover of his country muſt join with you in the hope, that in this threatening proſpect of our affairs, harmony and unanimity may pervade our councils, and our citizens at large.

I return with thanks, your kind and unfeigned wishes for my health and happiness in these trying times.

JOHN ADAMS.

To the PRESIDENT of the UNITED STATES.

SIR,

AT this critical period, when the feelings of every heart impressed with the sentiments of love and duty to its country, must be excited, we, the citizens of Dorchester county, take the liberty to address you upon the conduct which, as chief magistrate of the United States, you have pursued in our disagreeable differences with the French republic. We beg you to be assured that your attempts to restore harmony between the two nations on just and honorable terms, and also your firm assertion of the claims, rights and independence of our country, meet our most cordial approbation, and have secured our warmest gratitude.—We feel with indignation and resentment the insults and contempt, with which your offers of reconciliation and friendship have been treated; particularly as those offers were made, after our commerce had been harrassed and almost destroyed by the most wanton and lawless depredations—after our nation had been insulted by the most vile and insidious

attempts

attempts to overawe and dictate to our legally constituted authorities. Although we highly value the blessings of peace, yet under the protection of Heaven, we are determined to rely with full confidence on your well-tried patriotism and wisdom, firmly resolved to support with our lives and property, the honor, the liberty and independence of our country.

To the CITIZENS *of* DORCHESTER *County*.

GENTLEMEN,

YOUR unanimous address has been presented to me by your representative, Mr. Dennis.

When you express in terms of so much force and propriety, the feelings of your hearts, impressed with sentiments of love and duty to your country; when you assure me that my attempts to restore harmony between the United States and France, on just and honorable terms, and my firm assertion of the claims, rights and independence of our country, meet your cordial approbation, and have secured your warmest gratitude; when you express your feelings of indignation and resentment, at the insults and contempt with which our offers of reconciliation and friendship have been treated, particularly as these offers were made, after our commerce had been harrassed by wanton and lawless depredations, and our nation had been insulted by vile and insidious attempts to overawe and dictate to our legally constituted authorities; when you declare your determination to rely with full confidence on my endeavors, firmly resolved to support with your lives and fortunes, the honor, liberty and independence of our country, under the protection of Heaven—you penetrate my heart with gratitude for what concerns myself, and must receive the loud applause of the honest world for what concerns the public.

JOHN ADAMS.

From the INHABITANTS *of* HARFORD *County, to the* PRESIDENT, SENATE, *and House of* REPRESENTATIVES *in* CONGRESS.

ACTUATED by a sincere and ardent desire of peace with all the world, we have viewed with much satisfaction the measures taken by our Executive for an accommodation of the differences unhappily subsisting between this country and the French republic, and very much regret that they have not been met by a like disposition on the other part, and as it appears highly important at this momentous crisis, that the unanimity of our sentiments and determinations should appear

appear manifest.—We think proper to declare, that we are fully determined firmly to support, in all situations, our independence, and the government of our choice.

To the INHABITANTS *of* HARFORD *County*.

GENTLEMEN,

YOUR virtuous resolutions at Harford town, unanimously adopted, have been presented to me by your representative in Congress, Mr. Matthews.

The satisfaction you manifest, in the measures taken for an accommodation of differences subsisting between this country and the French republic, is very agreeable to me.

The determination to support, in all situations, your independence and the government of your choice, is worthy of freemen and faithful citizens; and the public declaration of such sentiments at this time, in order to shew the unanimity of the people, is good policy, as it tends to confirm the confidence of the whole nation in one another, and to increase its respectability and consideration with foreign nations.

JOHN ADAMS.

To JOHN ADAMS, PRESIDENT *of the* UNITED STATES *of* AMERICA.

SIR,

WE, the citizens of Caroline county, being sensible that the present state of our national affairs requires and demands our attention and unanimity, and that a uniformity of principles and sentiments are the chief essentials in the direction and welfare of government, being excited by those feelings, and sentiments of duty and love to our country, which, at such a crisis, cannot but impress the heart of every good citizen, beg leave to address you upon that conduct which you have, as chief magistrate of the United States, lately pursued to adjust and terminate our disagreeable and painful differences with the French republic.

We assure you, that we cordially unite in approbating those wise, just and moderate measures which you have adopted and pursued, to restore harmony and reconciliation between the two nations; and that you will, at all times find us ready to embrace with exclusive fondness, every wise and expedient measure of national security and defence.

With due resentment we feel the indign contempt and insults with which your late offers of friendship and reconciliation to the French republic have been treated; and we we are happy to find, that not only duty, but inclination, prompted you to proceed therein with wisdom, temper, and patriotic zeal.

Whilst we appreciate peace and tranquillity as the first of national blessings, and the end of every wise government; we shall ever unite to place the necessary barriers against the impulses of passion, the combination of foreign power, the intrigues of faction, the haste of folly, or the spirit of encroachment. With the gracious protection of the Supreme Ruler, and with a reliance on your wisdom and patriotism, we unanimously resolve firmly to maintain and support with our lives and properties, the honor, dignity and independence of our country.

To the CITIZENS *of* CAROLINE *County.*

GENTLEMEN,

YOUR address has been presented to me, as you desired, by your representative in Congress, Mr. Hindman.

The present state of our national affairs indeed demands the attention of every citizen, and uniformity of spirit will be our greatest security. With your sentiments of duty and love to your country, if they should be general and uniform throughout the nation, we may all have confidence in the

the gracious protection of the Supreme Ruler.

Your approbation of the measures of government is a great satisfaction.

I cannot agree with you, that tranquillity is always the first of national blessings---there are times and objects, which demand of men, and especially of freemen, the sacrifice of peace, property and life. Indeed there can be no peace, without uniting to place the necessary barriers against the impulses of passion, the insinuations of foreign influence, the intrigues of faction, the haste of folly and the spirit of encroachment.

JOHN ADAMS.

From the JUSTICES, *the* GRAND *and* PETIT JURORS, *and the* OFFICERS *of* TALBOT *County* COURT, *and of a numerous and respectable Body of the* PEOPLE *of the County, to the* PRESIDENT *of the* UNITED STATES.

SIR,

THE people of Talbot county, in the State of Maryland, impressed in common with their fellow-citizens, with a lively sense of the critical situation of their public affairs, feel it a duty which they owe to their country and themselves, to address to you the sentiments which the present occasion has inspired.

We

We had hoped that the moderation, wisdom and justice, with which the executive government of the United States hath conducted itself in its relations with foreign powers, would have secured us from a participation in the war which has desolated Europe: It is therefore with extreme concern that we view the alarming position, in which the nation is placed by the rapacious avarice and destructive projects of those who tyrannize over the people of France. But in the midst of this concern, we derive abundant consolation from reflecting, that the measures which you have pursued for removing subsisting differences with the French republic, have proceeded from a liberal and sincere disposition to restore harmony, and preserve the important interests of the United States, without sacrificing the honor or sovereignty of their government; and were ably and wisely calculated to attain these ends, had your negociations been reciprocated with that spirit of reconciliation and friendship, which her public agents have so often, but so perfidiously professed. We feel the keenest indignation in perceiving that these advances have been treated with unmerited contempt; and that the ambitious directors of this government, wholly abandoning the immutable principles of justice, and equally disregarding the law of nations and the faith of treaties, have wantonly per-

sisted

sisted in accumulating injuries upon the commerce and persons of our citizens, and in vilifying, by the most scandalous insults, the executive authority of the United States.

In such a state of things, it becomes indispensably necessary for a free people to express their feelings, and to vindicate their rights; and while we declare our entire confidence in your wisdom and integrity, we assure you, Sir, of our determination to support every measure, which the present crisis may demand, at the hazard of our lives and fortunes, and to destroy those malignant hopes which have been entertained from a vain belief, that the people of this country are at variance with their government.

Animated as we are by the love of peace, it is not without reluctance that we contemplate the calamities of war: but resolved to maintain the rights and independence of our country, without the enjoyment of which, peace would be only vassalage, we are fully prepared to await the events which may befal us; and if recourse must be had to arms, we shall trust, under Divine Providence, to the justice of our cause; And under such auspices, we are confident that the issue will be fortunate, and be rendered glorious by the wisdom and patriotism of the government, and by the courage and virtue of the people.

To

To the JUSTICES, *the* GRAND *and* PETIT JURORS *and* OFFICERS *of* TALBOT *County, and the numerous Body of* PEOPLE *of that County.*

GENTLEMEN,

THIS unanimous address from so respectable an assembly of citizens, of such various classes and denominations, conveying to me the sentiments which the present occasion has inspired, does me great honor.

You see that neither justice nor moderation can secure us from a participation in the war which has agitated Europe. The rapacious avarice and destructive projects of those who rule in France, have made war upon us already for years—a war all of one side, a war without reciprocity.

Our negociations have been conducted upon public and national principles and interests, not upon little projects of the private ambition, or avarice of individuals among the rulers. Our advances have been treated with unmerited contempt; the question now is, Will you reverse your maxims? and by gratifying the rapacity of rulers abroad, teach your own future rulers at home lessons of rapacity?

The executive authority of your country, you may depend upon it, will be vilified, by the most scandalous insults, by such rulers, as long as it is upright and pure.

Peace

Peace without independence, according to your own happy expression, would be vassalage.

JOHN ADAMS.

From the CITIZENS *of* ELKTON *and its vicinity, in* CECIL *County, to the* PRESIDENT *and* CONGRESS *of the* UNITED STATES.

LIVING under a constitution organized by the wisdom of our country, as the best adapted to the attainment of those objects which are the end of all rational government. A constitution alike inimical to anarchy and hereditary power, every public functionary deriving authority mediately or immediately from the people, we deem it sufficient, to command our support of the measures of administration, that the competent authorities decide.

Well satisfied that the citizens of the United States are firm in this principle, we learn with indignation that in a foreign country an opinion prevails, that the measures of this government may be defeated or embarrassed by the conflicting opinions of individuals. To repel this idea so degrading to Americans, and to evince to the world our determination on that point, we think it proper to declare, that we will by all the means in our power, support the decisions of the constituted

ſtituted authorities: Holding it our duty, as good citizens, to ſuffer no opinion of ours, on the ſubject of their meaſures, to impair our zeal for their ſupport,

The unjuſt aggreſſions of the French republic upon the commerce of this country, and their unprecedented conduct towards our envoys, call for this public declaration of our ſentiments,

Anxious for the peace of our country and the diminution of the public debt, whilſt we are tenacious of the honor, dignity and commercial rights of the nation, we are happy to find that the conduct of the Preſident of the United States in his endeavors to adjuſt the exiſting differences with France, has been ſuch as to merit and receive the cordial approbation of all the real friends of America.

To the CITIZENS *of* ELKTON *and its vicinity, in* CECIL *County.*

GENTLEMEN;

YOUR addreſs to the Preſident and Congreſs of the United States, has been preſented to me by your repreſentative in Congreſs, Mr. Matthews.

Under a conſtitution, organized by the wiſdom of the people, alike inimical to anarchy, and hereditary power, every public functionary deriving authority mediately or immediately from the people, there cannot be a greater absurdity in theory, than an opinion in a foreign country, that the measures of this government may be defeated or embarrassed by the conflicting opinions of individuals, nor can there be a greater affront, or more injurious reflection cast on representative governments; for if the principle were well founded, the necessary consequence would be, that the people are incapable of supporting a government of their own choice and fabric; and that government must be hereditary, in order to give it strength, to combine the public opinion, to draw together the wills and forces of the people. Your zeal therefore to repel this idea so degrading to Americans, is natural and well founded.

Your declaration that by all the means in your power, you will support the decisions of the constituted authorities, is in the character of the best of citizens.

There is not one of you, my fellow-citizens, more anxious for the diminution of the public debt, than myself; and a well regulated sinking fund may one day be resorted to, as a powerful engine for that purpose: But I fear we shall find a necessity of postponing this salutary operation in its full extent, to a time when the honor and safety

of

of the nation ſhall be better ſecured than at preſent.

Your approbation of my conduct is very precious to me, and deſerves my thanks.

JOHN ADAMS.

RESOLUTIONS *unanimouſly adopted by the* CITIZENS *of* GEORGETOWN.

I. THAT in the opinion of this meeting, the Executive of the United States, in their inſtructions to our miniſters in France, afford the moſt unequivocal evidence of a ſincere deſire to promote and perpetuate an honorable peace with the French republic.

II. That although peace with all nations is juſtly dear to this country, yet that the preſervation of its honor and independence is the firſt national object, and ought therefore to be conſidered infinitely more eſtimable.

III. That this meeting feel it a duty to expreſs in the ſtrongeſt terms, their confidence in the wiſdom, virtue and patriotiſm of the conſtituted authorities of their country—their reliance that at this eventful period, their deliberations will be influenced by a pure regard to the happineſs and proſperity of the nation :—And that, whatever difference of opinion may exiſt among us,

in

in regard to our internal and domestic regulations; still if the necessity of a solemn appeal to arms should be imposed upon us, America, so far from shewing herself a degraded and divided people, will exhibit to the world an example of unanimity and patriotism not to be exceeded.

IV. That the chairman of this meeting be instructed to forward to the representative of this district, a copy of these resolutions; with a request that he will communicate the same to the President and Congress of the United States.

To the CITIZENS *of* GEORGETOWN.

GENTLEMEN,

MR. CRAIK, the representative of your district, has presented to me, in your name, a copy of the resolutions passed at a numerous and respectable meeting of the citizens of Georgetown.

Your approbation of the instructions to our ministers to France; your estimation of the honor and independence of your country, as the first national object, and more estimable even than the blessings of peace; your confidence in the constituted authorities of your country, and in the unanimity and patriotism of your fellow-citizens, the American people, are honorable

to

to yourselves, the government and the nation; and the communication of them at this crisis, cannot fail to be agreeable to all, but the enemies of this country.

From the CITIZENS *of* BOHEMIA MANOR *and* SASSAFRAS NECK, *in* CECIL *County, to the* PRESIDENT *of the* UNITED STATES.

SIR,

AS a portion of the people of this government, participating in the advantages resulting from well-secured freedom, we cannot remain indifferent to the manifold injuries, which, in violation of a solemn treaty and the laws of nations, are daily inflicted on our fellow-citizens. Nor can we view with apathy the reiterated indignities and outrages offered to the government of our choice.

Although we are not engaged in commerce, we are sensible of its importance to our interests, as cultivators of the earth; we therefore consider ourselves bound by that consideration, as well as the obligation of mutual concession to our fellow-citizens who pursue commerce, to contribute to its protection. We also most firmly believe that the interests of the people and of the government, are as intimately blended as those of agriculture and commerce: and we hold all attempts to separate the one from the other, in utmost detestation.

If, as has been insultingly insinuated, or rather asserted, there is a faction in this government so lost to American feelings, as to espouse the unjust and arrogant pretensions of a foreign nation, we beg leave to assure you that we are not of that description. And we trust that very few will be found so unworthy the blessings they enjoy.

While we sincerely lament that the prudent and pacific steps taken by our chief magistrate to preserve peace, so desirable to all nations, are likely to fail of the wished for effect, we highly applaud the policy of such temperate proceedings. Seeing in them a sincere and ardent desire to promote and accelerate an accommodation with the republic of France, on terms compatible with the rights, duties, interests and honor of the nation, we are encouraged to place additional confidence in the integrity and wisdom of the constituted authorities; and the more readily to promise our willing aid in support of such measures as may be adopted by them in the present unhappy situation of our public concerns.

We pray you, Sir, to accept our best wishes for the prolongation of your life, hitherto so eminently distinguished for its usefulness and patriotism, and that it may be blessed

blessed with the enjoyment of every happiness.

To the Citizens *of* Bohemia Manor *and* Sassafrass Neck, *in* Cecil *County.*

GENTLEMEN,

I THANK you for this address. It would be unaccountable indeed, if any portion of a people, who acknowledge a participation in the advantages resulting from well secured freedom, could be indifferent to the manifold injuries which, in violation of a solemn treaty and the laws of nations, are daily inflicted on our fellow-citizens, or view with apathy the reiterated indignities and outrages offered to the government of their choice.

The importance of commerce to the interests of the cultivators of the earth, is so obvious, that at least as much zeal has apperred for its protection in the landed interests as the monied interest, in farmers as in merchants, in country citizens as in navigators.

If the interests of the people and of the government are not as intimately blended as those of agriculture and commerce in an elective government, in what other form can they be more so? Will those who attempt to separate the one from the other, pretend

pretend that in hereditary governments they are more so? or under military conquerors?

I believe with you that very few will be found so unworthy of the blessings they enjoy, as to espouse the unjust and arrogant pretensions of a foreign nation, yet we have found that a few venal presses, and unprincipled mercenaries have been able to raise loud clamors, produce much discontent, and threaten serious calamities.

The expressions of your satisfaction and confidence, as well as the promise of your willing aid, in support of such measures as may be adopted in the present unhappy situation of our public concerns, are very agreeable.

For your kind wishes for the prolongation of my life, I return you mine, for every blessing on you and posterity.

JOHN ADAMS.

VIRGINIA.

To the PRESIDENT *of the* UNITED STATES.

SIR,

AT this important moment, when imminent danger threatens us from abroad, the undersigned Young Men of Richmond, feel themselves

themselves impelled by that common sentiment, which now animates America, to express their fervent wishes for peace; but their determined resolution to support those measures of government, which are calculated to repel foreign aggressions, and to protect our country from injury and insult. We deem it the duty of every citizen, to support all those measures of government, which are constitutionally adopted: but impressed with a firm belief that the conduct of our government has been impartial as a neutral nation, that it has been faithful in its sacred observance of treaties, and that it has demonstrated its friendly disposition to an ancient ally, by offering that explanation of existing differences, which could alone restore harmony: our duty as citizens shall, on this occasion, be animated by the active energy of patriotic zeal.—It is much to be lamented, that separated as we are from the European world, we must still feel its agitations: It is much more to be lamented, that we should be reluctantly dragged into a contest with the French nation; a nation which once aided our fathers in a difficult and glorious struggle, and for whom we have been once taught to cherish something more than esteem and friendship. Our hearts too are still free to confess a veneration for the mighty effort which overturned the degrading despotism of royalty, and the multiplied

multiplied mischiefs of their political system; but when we see the enthusiasm for liberty, extinguished by an ambition which grasps at the domination of the world; when we behold them intoxicated with success, proudly dictating to unwilling nations, and subjugating those who are not submissive slaves, or the ready instruments of their future domination—that bosom which once glowed with exultation, for the triumphs of Frenchmen, now burns with no less indignation at their flagitious conduct, their present injuries and insults—injuries too many and too aggravated, for silence and inaction.

It is a cause of infinite regret that the repeated offers to negociate, on our part, should be treated with disdain; that in sullen silence, the rulers of France should turn a deaf ear to the voice of justice and friendship, or indirectly menace us with vengeance, by presenting to our view those unfortunate and degraded people, who have already been forced to bend beneath their yoke. We feel, however, a pleasing consolation, that you, Sir, have exhibited to the world, the most unequivocal testimonials of the upright intentions of our government, and that the mind of man cannot resist the evidence which it discloses of a friendly, just and rigorously impartial conduct.

It is our wish, and we believe it to be your's, that the calamities of war should be averted:

averted by every mean, consistent with the honor, dignity, and rights of an independent nation: but if this evil, which we deprecate, should be our lot, the firmness of freemen will be sustained by a belief, that moderation and justice will consecrate the sword, which necessity draws. We repose confidence in the wisdom and virtue of the constituted authorities, and permit us to assure you, Sir, that we shall be ever ready to lend our aid, in vindication of our violated rights, and that our endeavors, though weak, shall be ever ready to lend our aid, in vindication of our violated rights, and that our endeavors, though weak, shall be zealously joined with the rest of our fellow-citizens, in supporting the liberty and independence of our country, against the unjust attacks of the French nation, or any other power on earth.

To the YOUNG MEN *of* RICHMOND.

GENTLEMEN,

AN address, so respectful to me, so faithful to the nation, and true to its government, from so honorable a portion of the Young Men of Richmond, cannot fail to be very acceptable to me.

You will not take offence, I hope, at my freedom, however, if I say, that if you had been taught to cherish in your hearts, an esteem

esteem and friendship for France, it would have been enough; more than these toward any foreign power, had better be reserved.

It might have been as well for us in America, whose distance is so great, and whose knowledge of France, and her government, was so imperfect, to have suspended our veneration, for the mighty effort which overturned royalty, until we should have seen all degrading despotism at an end in the country, and something more consistent with virtue, equality, liberty and humanity substituted in its place—Hitherto the progress has been from bad to worse.

The conduct of the French government towards us, is of a piece with their behaviour to their own citizens, and a great part of Europe. Your sensibility to their insults and injuries to your country, is very becoming, and your resolution to resist them, do you honor.

A fresh insult is now offered to all America, and especially to her government, in the arbitrary dismission of two of their envoys, with scornful intimations of capricious prejudices against them—But I am weary of enumerating insults and injuries.

JOHN ADAMS.

To

RESOLUTIONS *adopted by the* INHABITANTS *of the Town of* ALEXANDRIA.

I. THAT the proſpect of an impending rupture with the republic of France, is one which is deeply to be deplored; and that war and all meaſures of conflict that lead directly to hoſtilities with that or any other nation, are only to be juſtified by cauſes which affect our national independence, but that when theſe exiſt, and are not to be averted by means of amicable negociation, arms become the natural, equitable and indiſpenſable reſort.

II. That the meaſures which have been adopted and purſued by the Executive of the United States, to obtain retribution for injuries, and to reſtore harmony between us and the French republic, have been truly wiſe and patriotic; the event having abundantly proved, that on the part of France there exiſts a corrupt adminiſtration, to whom a further application on the principles of juſtice, muſt continue to be nugatory.

III. That while a hope is cheriſhed that ſome foreign political event may ſoon take place, to obviate preſent appearances and diſſipate the gloom of war, it is expedient nevertheleſs, for the government of this country, to adopt with promptitude effectual meaſures of defence; to act like the rulers of a free and independent nation, whose situation and internal resources enable it to scourge every invader of its rights or territories, and that in conformity with these sentiments, the citizens of Alexandria promise a faithful co-operation with the administration and cheerful and prompt compliance with any degree or mode of taxation which shall be deemed necessary or expedient.

IV. That the foregoing resolutions be published in the Alexandria newspapers, and that a copy of them be transmitted to the President of the United States, the President of the Senate, and Speaker of the House of Representatives.

V. That a committee be appointed to prepare an address to the President of the United States, inclosing the foregoing resolutions.

From the COMMITTEE *of the* INHABITANTS *of the Town of* ALEXANDRIA, *to the* PRESIDENT *of the* UNITED STATES.

SIR,

THE citizens of Alexandria, viewing with the liveliest apprehensions the alarming situation of our political differences with the republic of France, as detailed in the communications of our envoys at Paris to the Secretary

Secretary of State, and desirous of evincing their attachment to the government of their country, and a virtuous indignation at any attempt to infringe its national sovereignty, have commissioned us to transmit to you the inclosed resolutions expressive of their sentiments upon subjects so important and interesting to the peace, dignity and prosperity of the United States. We have seen with anxious regret, the gradual dissolution of those ties of gratitude and affection, which have so long attached America to the interests of France: but when that affection is violated by the grossest injuries; when an expression of gratitude becomes our reproach, and we are smarting under the lash of unprovoked aggressions; when every attempt at amicable negociation has been frustrated, it becomes the indispensable duty of a free people to vindicate the insulted honor of its national character.

We embrace, Sir, with peculiar satisfaction, this favorable opportunity of expressing to you, the warm acknowledgments of a grateful people for your truly wise and patriotic exertions to preserve the tranquillity of your country. The measures adopted and pursued by the Executive of the United States, meet our warmest approbation; and though many attempts have been made to separate us from the government of our choice, and the difference of political sentiment

ment has been the mean employed for that purpose, yet be assured we will ever repel with unanimity and energy, every effort of a foreign power to diminish our rights as an independent nation. We take a pride in expressing to you, Sir, our entire approbation of the rectitude and integrity of your administration. We are pleased to see those virtues and talents so often exercised for the benefit of your country in the late revolutionary contest, again exerted in the discharge of the arduous duties of the first magistrate of the Union. Accept, Sir, our sincere and ardent wishes for your public prosperity and private happiness.

From the YOUNG MEN *of the County of* GREENSVILLE, *to the* PRESIDENT *of the* UNITED STATES.

SIR,

TO assure you of our concurrence, at this time, with the measures pursued by you, in support of our independence, is not the purpose of this address. It is to claim a share in the defence of our country, and once more shew the contrast between the defenders of liberty, and the hirelings of despotism. We trust we are not degenerated from our fathers who obtained our liberties, and be it our care to preserve the fair inheritance inviolate.

Suffer

Suffer us to assure you, that you have only to point out the mode, and our lives now, as they ever have been, shall willingly be sacrificed in the defence of our liberties and government.

We regret our distance from Philadelphia, as by that mean we are deprived of the happiness of assuring you personally, of our readiness, under your command, to take up arms in defence of our constitution.

Permit us too, to congratulate you on the hearty concurrence of our brothers of Philadelphia; and thus may you, as long as our country shall demand the exertion of your abilities, receive in the most ample manner, the sentiments and good wishes of every American.

To the YOUNG MEN *of* GREENSVILLE.

GENTLEMEN,

YOUR address is in a style to convince me, that you are not degenerated from the wisdom and virtues of your fathers, and that you will preserve the fair inheritance, which they defended with so much success.

The claim you advance to share in the defence of your country, the sacrifices you offer to make, and the applause you bestow on your brothers of Philadelphia, are honorable to your characters.

If your diſtance had not prevented, I ſhould have ſeen you in Philadelphia with pleaſure.

JOHN ADAMS.

RESOLUTIONS *unanimouſly adopted by a* COMMITTEE *compoſed of a* DEPUTATION *from each* MILITIA COMPANY *of the Forty-eighth* REGIMENT *in the County of* BOTETOURT.

I. IT is the opinion of this meeting, that the Preſident of the United States not only poſſeſſes, but is entitled to the confidence of the people of this part of the United States.

II. That it is with extreme regret, we ſee the attempts of ſome of our citizens to detract from his real merit, and propagate the idea of diſaffection to an excellent government and its adminiſtration.

III. That while we lament any cauſe which would tend to interrupt the tranquillity, proſperity and independence, which, under Divine Providence, we are permitted at preſent to enjoy, we will with firmneſs repel any attempts to wreſt thoſe bleſſings from us, from whatſoever quarter they may proceed. And that although it is our wiſh to be at peace with all the world, more particularly with the French republic, we ſhall prefer

fer hostilities even with that nation, to a proftration of our rights, and that ftate of national degradation to which they have lately attempted to reduce us.

IV. That our chairman do draft an addrefs to the Prefident of the United States, in the fpirit of the foregoing refolutions, and expreffive of the high fenfe we entertain of his firmnefs, integrity and patriotifm, and that he caufe the faid refolutions and addrefs to be printed in fuch of the Gazettes of the United States as he may think proper.

To the PRESIDENT *of the* UNITED STATES.

SIR,

THE attention of the people of this county, awaked by the alarming crifis of American affairs, has been directed to the meafures of your adminiftration; and they declare with an unanimous voice, that you have merited and poffefs their entire confidence. They behold with with extreme regret, the attempts of fome of their fellow-citizens to propagate an idea of difaffection to an excellent government and its adminiftration; and this regret is accompanied with indignation, when they perceive that it has encouraged in a foreign country, the plan of degrading our republic, from its independent ftation. They prize moft highly the

bleffings

blessings of peace and prosperity, which, by the Divine favor, they at present enjoy; but considering them as the fruits of the happy government of their choice, they will repel any attack upon its independence, from whatever quarter it may proceed. It is their wish to cultivate peace with the whole world, and more particularly with the French republic; but they cannot consent for this object, to sacrifice the honor and independence of the nation, without which peace must be precarious and unblessed.

Permit us to assure you, Sir, that we admire the consistency of your character; and are pleased to see the same firmness, integrity and patriotism at the present day, which you so eminently displayed in the great crisis of the American revolution.

To the COMMITTEE *composed of a* DEPUTATION *from each* MILITIA COMPANY *of the Forty-eighth* REGIMENT *in the County of* BOTETOURT.

GENTLEMEN,

A COPY of your unanimous resolutions together with an address, signed by your chairman, has been presented to me by one of your representatives in Congress, Mr. Evans.

The

The confidence of the people of Virginia, or any such respectable portion of them, is peculiarly agreeable to me, as it evinces a tendency to a restoration of that harmony and union, which I well remember to have once existed, and which was so auspicious to the American cause, but which has been apparently interrupted since the commencement of the Federal government.

It is scarcely possible that I should ever read a sentence more delightful to my heart, than those words, "We admire the consistency of your character, and are pleased to see the same firmness, integrity and patriotism at the present day, so eminently displayed in the great crisis of the American revolution."

JOHN ADAMS.

To the PRESIDENT *of the* UNITED STATES.

SIR,

AT a moment when foreign dangers threaten our peace, and when these dangers originate in an opinion that our government and our people are divided in sentiment, and opposed in interest, we, inhabitants of the borough of Norfolk, feel ourselves impelled by every consideration of honor, as men, and integrity, as citizens, to express our unshaken confidence in the measures of

our

our government, and our unimpaired attachment to the principles of our conſtitution.

In reviewing thoſe meaſures of our government, which are the avowed cauſes of the unfriendly conduct which the French republic has practiſed towards us, we feel an honeſt pride in expreſſing our opinion, that impropriety or cenſure cannot juſtly attach themſelves to thoſe meaſures.

In examining the ſteps which have been purſued to obtain an amicable adjuſtment of exiſting differences, we ſee with pleaſure a liberal, candid and ſincere diſpoſition on the part of our government, to relinquiſh every ſecondary conſideration for the maintenance of peace; we regret that thoſe diſpoſitions have not been met with ſentiments equally pacific, with a temper equally conciliatory and accommodating on the part of France.

While we avow the friendly intereſt which we have formerly taken in the affairs of France, we reject with honeſt indignation her inadmiſſible demands; we ſpurn with manly pride the imputations of diſunion and diſaffection to our government, on which theſe demands were founded.

We deprecate a war, as pregnant with evils to all countries, and particularly inimical to the intereſts of the United States; but we are at the ſame time determined not to purchaſe

purchase peace at the price of that national character and individual security, without which, peace ceases to be either honorable or desirable.

While, therefore, we hope that a returning sense of justice and moderation on the part of France, will terminate our disagreements by friendly explanation, and honorable reparation ; while we rely that our own government will not cease to avoid war, by every mean, consistent with our national honor, and compatible with our national interest, we yet trust that measures of defence will be immediately adopted, and that our country will be prepared to meet every possible event.

Should these measures, defensive in their nature, and prompted by a necessary regard to our unquestionable rights, be considered as indicative of a hostile disposition to the French republic, the government of the United States stands acquitted to its citizens and the world. Providence alone can determine the issue : we pledge ourselves that it will be fortunate so far as our steady cooperation and support of the government can render it so.

To the PRESIDENT *of the* UNITED STATES.

SIR,

WE the ſubſcribers, inhabitants of the county of Middleſex, in the State of Virginia, now offer our moſt unfeigned approbation of the wiſe ſyſtem which governs your adminiſtration in purſuing the ſame principle of neutrality that the late Preſident Waſhington adopted at the commencement of this war among the European powers, a principle that hath been adhered to on the part of the United States, with the moſt inviolable faith. You have evinced that ſoundneſs of judgment, which every man who knew your character as a ſtateſman anticipated, when the voice of America called you to the ſupreme adminiſtration of theſe States: Scanning your conduct ſince your appointment, with the jealous eye that vigilant freedom ſhould ever carry over executory magiſtracy, we find it difficult to determine whether more to admire your wiſdom, or your firmneſs and moderation.

The late diſpatches from our envoys at Paris, and the inſtructions given by the Executive, ſhew beyond the poſſibility of doubt, that it is your ardent wiſh to recur to every expedient to heal the differences, that aggreſſions unprovoked, have occaſioned between France and theſe United States; and

that

that your moderation carried you to every length to accomplish this object, short of the resignation of the independence these States had acquired, after a long struggle, by their courage, their treasure, and their blood.

After these dispatches and instructions received the fulness of publicity, and exhibited to the conviction of impartial America, the prudent measures that actuated the President of the United States, we flattered ourselves all party divisions in every branch of our public councils would be at once extinguished; but, though this desirable result has not as yet as immediately ensued as we expected, we are happy to find the people at large in every part of these States, in proportion as they are informed and enlightened on this greatly interesting object, and see the true drift of the conduct of the supreme executive power, have come to this determination—To support their country in all its rights of independence, at whatever expense of treasure, and peril of person, sooner than submit without a struggle to the wanton exactions, the imperious mandates, and the injurious treatment of any foreign nation.

To the INHABITANTS *of the County of* MIDDLESEX.

GENTLEMEN,

I THANK you for this address, presented to me by your representative in Congress, Mr. New.

The principle of neutrality, has indeed been maintained on the part of the United States with inviolable faith, notwithstanding every embarrassment and provocation, both of injury and insult, until we have been forced out of it, by an actual war made upon us, though not manfully declared.

For reasons that are obvious to all the world, you may easily imagine, that every manifestation of candor towards me from any part of Virginia, must be peculiarly agreeable—the handsome expressions of your approbation deserve my thanks. Every thing has been done, short of a resignation of our independence—a resignation of our *independence!* I blush to write the words; there would be as much sense in speaking of a resignation of the independence of France or Germany, or Russia: We are a nation as much established as any of them, and as able to maintain our sovereignty, absolute and unlimited by sea and land, as any of them.

It is too much to expect, that all party divisions will be done away, as long as there are rival States and rival individuals; all

we

we can reasonably hope is, and this we may confidently expect, that no State or individual, to gratify its ambition, will enlist under foreign banners.

JOHN ADAMS.

To the PRESIDENT of the UNITED STATES.

SIR,

THE inhabitants of the county of Bedford, and State of Virginia, beg leave, at this important crisis, to join the general voice of their fellow citizens in other parts of the United States, in expressing to you their sincere approbation of the measures which have been adopted by the Executive, to preserve the blessings of peace to this country, and particularly to restore harmony with the French republic; we reflect with gratitude, on the earnest solicitude, and successful endeavors of your illustrious predecessor, to avoid a participation in the destructive consequences of an European war; and we acknowledge, with pleasure, a correspondent sentiment, on a review of the wise, firm and patriotic measures of your administration.

Although we deprecate war with any nation, and deplore the prospect that now threatens our peace, yet under such auspices,

ces, and relying on the unanimity of the people; the justice of our cause, and the protection of Divine Providence, we look forward with confidence to a favorable issue, even with that nation, who, flushed with victory, has insolently threatened our country with the humiliating fate of many of those powers she has conquered. The exercise of foreign influence in the United States, is so degrading, that every American, we trust, will repel, with indignation, any attempts of the kind. For ourselves, we disdain the spirit that would bend to a mean subserviency to the views of any power whatever.

Feeling an unlimited attachment to and confidence in the government of the United States, we do not hesitate to declare our determination to support, to the utmost of our power, every measure deemed necessary for the defence, honor and interest of our country.

And we implore the Supreme Ruler of events to continue your strength of body and mind, so that you may terminate the present unhappy situation of our affairs with honor to yourself, and with glory to these United States.

To JOHN ADAMS, President of the United States.

SIR,

YOUR fellow-citizens of the county of Westmoreland cannot, at this important crisis, withhold their offering of gratitude and respect to their chief magistrate, as well to assure him of their unshaken decision at all times, and on all occasions to maintain inviolate the independence of their country, as to relieve the reputation of the American nation from the unfounded aspersions which the agents of a foreign country have asserted in support of wrongs inflicted, in contempt of a solemn treaty of friendship, on our unoffending peaceable fellow-citizens, and of demands made on the honor and purse of our country.

The declaration that our people are hostile to a government made by themselves, for themselves, and conducted by themselves, is an insult, malignant in its nature and extensive in its mischief: While it supports the opinion that the efforts of the accusing nation have, under the cover of amity, promoted the deepest injury, it shews too that on the success of this favorite scheme do they chiefly rely for the execution of their wicked projects. On our enemy the acknowledgment pours down shame and confusion, and is to our countrymen a mon-

 itory

itory lesson, from which great good we trust will be derived.

That freemen should differ in opinion concerning the measures of their government, is not only to be expected, but is even to be desired, when obedient to law, and guided by love of country: but differences like these (and we believe that, generally speaking, only such have existed among us) while they prove the general happiness, may be considered as sure pledges of united efforts to defend that government from insult and injury, under whose wing all participate alike in the felicity it diffuses. If we should unfortunately hold in our bosom citizens bearing the American name, and destitute of the American heart, they must be few in number; and wise laws, firmly executed, will speedily cure every evil flowing from this source: To the wisdom of Congress we look for the remedy, and in your paternal vigilance and immoveable firmness we rely for its effectual application.

When our forefathers exchanged their native country for the wilderness of America, devotion to their God, obedience to the principles of morality, love of liberty guided by love of order, were their governing principles: This precious inheritance our fathers cherished with sincere affection; and in a late awful trial, to the influence of these

first-rate

first-rate rules on our infant nation, may with truth be chiefly ascribed the glorious issue of our common toils and common dangers. That issue we hold in trust for our posterity, and that trust we will never forfeit. Since that period we have grown strong by union. Where is the nation that can coerce United Columbia into submission? The sun has not yet shone upon it.

We love peace—we hate war; but we prize our honor too highly to wish the continuance of the first, or to turn from the perils of the last, with a degraded name. We believe too (and in this belief, past as well as present experience justifies us) that the surest way to preserve peace, is to be prepared for war.

Your sincere and dignified endeavors to conciliate differences, to obtain restitution for wrongs, and your determination to sacrifice all secondary considerations on the altar of peace; sheds new lustre on your well-earned fame, and adds a new title to your established claim on the admiration and gratitude of your fellow-citizens.

Conciliation being rejected, war continued, one course only was left by which national disgrace could be instantly arrested, and national existence permanently maintained. That happy course you have taken with decision, frankness and fortitude; we cannot

cannot hesitate in the part becoming us to act. In peace we obey the laws; we foster the union of the States; we inspire our children with love of virtue, of their country, and their God: In war we know but one additional obligation—to die in the last ditch, or uphold our nation. This sacred duty we will teach by our example; and in full reliance on the justice of our cause, we are prepared to meet every event to which we may be exposed, with a resolution deserving victory.

To the Almighty Ruler of nations we humbly commend our country and our President, and we implore him to pour upon them the continual dew of his blessing.

To JOHN ADAMS, PRESIDENT *of the* UNITED STATES.

SIR,

AT a crisis when the sovereignty of our country is assailed; when demands are made upon us by a foreign nation, altogether incompatible with our honor and independence and when in case of a refusal to accede to those demands, even our national existence is threatened: when we have reason to believe that an opinion has gone forth (which has contributed to produce this conduct) that we are a people divided among ourselves

ourſelves by faction and party ſpirit, diſtracted by feuds and animoſities, and ſeparated from our government, both by opinion and intereſt ;—we, the inhabitants of the county of Accomack in the State of Virginia, convened in full meeting at the court-houſe of the ſaid county, by previous public notice, feel ourſelves called upon by duty, as well as inclination, to declare, and we do unanimouſly declare, our entire approbation of the meaſures which have hitherto been purſued by our government—our confident reliance that ſuch only will in future be purſued as will comport with the honor and intereſt of our country—and our unceaſing attachment to the principles of our conſtitution.

We declare our conviction that our government has manifeſted a moſt earneſt deſire to preſerve peace with all nations, particularly with the French republic ; that upon a fair and candid review of the conduct of our government, we diſcover nothing which ought to have given umbrage to that republic, or which can in any wiſe juſtify her numerous aggreſſions on the perſons and properties of our citizens, in direct violation of the laws of nations, and in contravention of her exiſting treaties with us : and that even ſince thoſe multiplied cauſes of diſſatisfaction have exiſted, the meaſures purſued towards that country have been marked by a

ſpirit

ſpirit of mildneſs and conciliation, ſuch as ought to have realized our reaſonable hopes, that they would prove ſucceſsful.

It is with the utmoſt concern and regret, therefore, that we perceive thoſe efforts to maintain harmony, and to avert the calamities of war with that republic, are likely to prove abortive, and that our advances towards an amicable adjuſtment of exiſting differences have not been met by a like friendly and pacific diſpoſition on the part of the French nation, but that conditions have been eſſayed to be impoſed upon our country, which they have ſometimes called their ſiſter republic, that would be degrading to a free nation, and ſuch as we do not heſitate to reject with indignation.

Although we view war as particularly injurious to the intereſts of our country, yet we conſider it as an evil of leſs magnitude than national degradation. While therefore, we would fain indulge a hope, that the French republic may return to a ſenſe of juſtice, by withholding further acts of hoſtility and outrage, by making reparation for thoſe already committed, and by cloſing with overtures made for the reſtoration of harmony and a friendly intercourſe between the two countries, upon the broad baſis of equal right and reciprocal benefit;—we truſt our country will be prepared to meet the

the contrary event, and to assert and maintain her rights with firmness, even at the expense of war with all its horrors.

We promise cheerfully to co-operate in whatever measures those entrusted with the administration of our government shall deem conducive to the interests, and consistent with the honor of the nation: and we pledge our lives, our fortunes, and all we hold dear, upon the success of the issue.

To the INHABITANTS *of* ACCOMACK *County*.

GENTLEMEN,

I PRAY you to accept my thanks for your unanimous address, replete with sentiments truly American.

Your conviction that your government has manifested a most earnest and sincere desire to preserve peace with all nations, particularly with the French republic; your declaration that upon a candid review of the conduct of your government, you can discover nothing which ought to have given umbrage to that republic, or which can in any wise justify her numerous aggressions on the persons and properties of our citizens, in direct violation of the law of nations, and in contravention of her existing treaties with us—ought to give entire satisfaction to the government.

Your

Your concern and regret, that those efforts to maintain harmony, have proved abortive, are natural and common to you and me, and all our fellow-citizens, but can be of no use; instead of dwelling on our regrets, we must explore our resources. Although we may view war as particularly injurious to the interests of our country, Providence may intend it for our good, and we must submit. That it is a less evil than national dishonor, no man of sense and spirit will deny.

I have no hope that the French republic will soon return to a sense of justice.

Your promise to co-operate in whatever measures government may deem conducive to the interests, and consistent with the honor of the nation, and your pledge of your lives and fortunes, and all you hold dear, upon the success of the issue, are in the true spirit of men, of freemen, of Americans and genuine republicans.

JOHN ADAMS.

To JOHN ADAMS, PRESIDENT *of the* UNITED STATES.

SIR,

WE, the subscribers, a committee appointed by a respectable meeting of the inhabitants of Harrison county, in the Commonwealth

wealth of Virginia, holden at Clarksburgh, for the purpose of expressing their sentiments of the measures pursued by our government with respect to France—beg leave to assure you, that although among the last in addressing, we are not less attached to our government—a government calculated to ensure liberty and happiness to its citizens. In plain undisguised language, we do not hesitate to declare, that the measures you have taken to promote a good understanding, harmony and peace, between this country and France, appear to us becoming your character, and deserving our confidence. But her refusal to meet your condescending plans of accommodation, except upon the condition of an advance of money, evinces on her part a spirit of avarice and tyranny, unknown among civilized nations, in modern times; and evidently shews, that having become haughty and arbitrary by her successes, she means to act as did ancient Rome.

But, Sir, we can congratulate you on her disappointment, in an essential matter, upon which she calculated highly—The want of attachment to our government, and a division of sentiment in regard to that nation. With infinite satisfaction must every true American view, that the alarm of war has silenced all essential differences in opinion, and a union of sentiment appears to prevail universally throughout our land; and the day, we trust, is not far distant, when the odious distinction of *aristocrat* and *democrat* will be done away, and as one man we shall unite in the common cause. Had the desired object been obtained, upon the just and honorable terms proposed, we would have cheerfully united with the warmest advocates for peace, the most lively expressions of mutual congratulation.—We cannot forget, that the very genius and principles of the religion we profess, teaches us, as much as possible, to live peaceably with all men; yet we conceive it not possible to maintain a friendly correspondence, or even to be at peace with a nation, that under the mask of philanthropy commits the greatest cruelties, exercises the most despotic sway, destroys all order, and establishes impiety by law. Viewing the matter in this light, we do not wonder, that the most just, wise and patriotic overtures of peace with the French nation, have proved abortive. Be assured, therefore, although war may be the consequence of your steady attachment to our real interests, we would rather immediately be called forth into the field of battle, in support of such measures as the constituted authorities of the Union shall adopt, for the defence and maintenance of our national independence, than enjoy a momentary delusive *purchased peace*.

We

We truſt, that the God of our armies will aid us in defending, what we thankfully enjoy as his gift—and impute the guilt of offenſive war, to thoſe, who have rejected the offers of peace; who, without provocation, have plundered us on the high ſeas; who have endeavoured to ſubvert our government by the mean arts of ſeduction, and even now threaten us with revenge, unleſs we will ſuccour them in their ambitious views of *univerſal domination.*

May that God who has graciouſly placed you at the head of our national affairs, long preſerve your life, and make you the happy inſtrument of conducting us with ſafety through this impending ſtorm.

To the INHABITANTS *of* HARRISON *County.*

GENTLEMEN,

I HAVE received with great pleaſure your addreſs, from your committee. The attachment you profeſs to our government, calculated as it is, to enſure liberty and happineſs to its citizens, is commendable. Your declarations, in plain and undiſguiſed language, that the meaſures which have been taken to promote a good underſtanding, peace and harmony, between this country and France, are becoming my character and deſerving your confidence, is a great encouragement

agement to me. With you, I see with infinite satisfaction, that the alarming prospect of a war, which is seen to be just and necessary, has silenced all essential differences of opinions, and that a union of sentiments appears to prevail very generally throughout our land. I believe, however, that the distinction of *aristocrat* and *democrat*, however odious and pernicious it may be rendered, by political artifice at particular conjunctures, will never be done away, as long as some men are taller, and others shorter, some wiser, and others sillier, some more virtuous, and others more vicious, some richer, and others poorer. The distinction is grounded on unalterable nature, and human wisdom can do no more than reconcile the parties by equitable establishments and equal laws, securing, as far as possible, to every one, his own. The distinction was intended by nature, for the order of society, and the benefit of mankind. The parties ought to be like the sexes, mutually beneficial to each other. And woe will be to that country, which supinely suffers malicious demagogues to excite jealousies, foment prejudices, and stimulate animosities between them.

I adore with you the genius and principles of that religion, which teaches, as much as possible, to live peaceably with all men; yet it is impossible to be at peace with *injustice* and *cruelty*, with *fraud* and *violence*, with

despotism,

despotism, *anarchy* and *impiety*. A *purchased* peace would continue no longer than you continued to pay; and the field of battle at once, is infinitely preferable to a course of perpetual and unlimited contribution.

Deeply affected with your prayers for the continuance of my life, I can only say, that my age and infirmities scarcely allow me a hope of being the happy instrument of conducting you through the impending storm.

JOHN ADAMS.

From the INHABITANTS *of the County of* CAMPBELL, *to His Excellency* JOHN ADAMS, PRESIDENT *of the* UNITED STATES.

SIR,

IF the American government dare not make treaties with other nations without the consent of France; if the President of the United States dare not communicate to Congress the state of the Union without consulting France; if we are to be plundered of millions by the French, and dare not resent it; if we are to bribe the most corrupt government under the sun, and become tributary to it; in fine, if we are to submit to insults without number, or injuries unbounded, and keep our mouths sealed, and our hands

hands chained behind us;—delusive indeed is our independence, and in vain have our ancestors fought and spilled the best blood of America.

Peace to us is truly desirable; we wish to enjoy it; but France seems determined to break down that vine and fig-tree, under which we were reposing.

America, and all the world, except France, can vouch for the sincerity of your exertions, to preserve an honorable peace; and we verily believe that the whole tenor of your administration has been bottomed on a sincere wish for the real welfare of our common country, aided by eminent talents and the most solid judgment.

As well wishers to all mankind, we should feel abundant pleasure in seeing the French people peaceably settled under a well organized government; but the name or nature of it is to us a matter of indifference, if they should be satisfied;—but our good wishes do not carry us so far as to be willing to abandon to them one particle of our independence, to submit quietly to their intrigues, or to be drawn from that path which we have a right to pursue. We love our government, and believe it to be the best under the sun; we place the highest confidence in the constituted authorities, and trust that the Executive will pursue such measures

measures as may best conduce to our welfare. It would be superfluous to add, that our persons and property are ready to protect our independence;—and that you may long continue its firm supporter, is the sincere wish of the citizens of Campbell.

From the INHABITANTS *of* SHEPHERD'S TOWN *and its vicinity, in the County of* BERKLEY, *to* JOHN ADAMS, PRESIDENT *of the* UNITED STATES.

SIR,

IN the present eventful period, when unremitting depredations are committed on our commerce, wanton cruelty exercised on our seamen, the general government traduced, the Executive vilified, and our very existence threatened by the French government, and that through the means of our own citizens; we esteem it a duty we owe to our country, to ourselves and to posterity, publicly to declare our sentiments, and to offer every support in our power to the constituted authorities. We therefore declare to you, Sir, that we are of opinion you have done every thing that under the existing circumstances could be done, with due regard to the general safety, true honor and essential interest of the United States, to cultivate a good understanding and preserve

peace

peace with the French nation. And that through the unexampled perfidy and unparalleled baseness of the conduct of that government towards us, nothing further can be attempted consistent with the maxims that constitute the basis of our national sovereignty. And we further declare to you, Sir, and to the world, that your administration of the executive government in all respects, meets our most cordial and hearty approbation; and should a storm await and our enemies assail us, while by the blessing of Providence we have ample resources, and a chief magistrate at the helm deservedly possessing our confidence, while we have a right to hope for the energetic concurrence of the legislative branches, and can appeal to Heaven for the justness of our cause, we fear no consequences, but are determined in any event to support the government of our own choice with our lives and fortunes.

To the INHABITANTS *of* SHEPHERD'S TOWN *and its vicinity, in the County of* BERKLEY.

GENTLEMEN,

THE generous sentiments of approbation and confidence conveyed in this nervous address, command my particular respect.

I had never until lately, any expectation, that I should live to see unremitted depredations

dations committed on our commerce, wanton cruelties exercifed on our feamen, our general government traduced, the executive authority vilified, and our very exiftence threatened, through the means of our citizens, or any other, with impunity. I had no fufpicion indeed, that mankind would ever have taken it into their heads, to try over again, experiments which had been a million times tried, and always found evil.

I am happy in your opinion, that every thing has been done, under the exifting circumftances, that could be done by me, with a due regard to the general fafety, true honor and effential interefts of the United States. With you I clearly agree, that nothing further can be attempted, confiftently with the maxims that conftitute the bafis of our national fovereignty.

Your cordial approbation of my adminiftration of the executive government, in all refpects is highly honorable and affecting to me.

Should our enemies affail us at home, you will have no reafon to doubt of the energetic concurrence of the legiflative branches, whofe knowledge of our ample refources, muft give them all neceffary firmnefs; whofe perfuafion of the juftice of our caufe, will enable them to make the laft appeal when neceffary, and whofe American hearts will

prompt

prompt them to support their country, with their lives and fortunes, in common with their fellow-citizens.

JOHN ADAMS.

NORTH-CAROLINA.

To the PRESIDENT *of the* UNITED STATES.

SIR,

THE inhabitants of the town of Newbern, find an excuse for the freedom they exercise in this address to you, in the critical and alarming situation of the government, in a common concern for the preservation of its honor and independence, and in the warm approbation they entertain of your conduct since you have filled the office of chief magistrate of the United States.—You were called to it, Sir, at a crisis fraught with difficulty and danger, when neither the improved skill in the management of affairs, nor the purest integrity of intention could ensure an entire exemption from censure—At a crisis when the honor, interest and happiness of the United States, required that a distinct and impartial neutrality should be fairly maintained with all foreign powers, but which an artful and insidious set of men at the head of the government of the French republic, were laboring

laboring to interrupt and destroy—Abroad it required a constant exertion of the most wary and active penetration, to elude the toils they had set for it,--—and at home, where you had a right to look for a cordial support, and a zealous and unanimous co-operation, you were forced to sustain your measures against the efforts of a deluded enthusiasm, propagated in the minds of some of our fellow-citizens, by an ill-grounded attachment to the French cause. But with a steady perseverance and exemplary firmness of mind which no obstacles could weary, nor misrepresentations discourage, you have persisted in a regular and stedfast course of measures happily adjusted to the promotion of the honor of our national character, the advancement of our national prosperity and the preservation of our national rights—And it may be the felicity and the boast of the citizens of the United States, that in the series of these various and critical events, the firmness and independency of your mind never once deserted you, and that all the steps you have taken have been guided by wisdom, upon a clear and judicious knowledge of the characters with whom you had to deal, and upon a jealous and anxious regard for the honor, happiness and independence of the government.

Now that the hostile and views and nefarious designs of the French republic towards the

the government of the United States have been expofed by the publication of the communications from our envoys, the love of our common country will produce a cordial unanimity of fentiment ; and whatever may be the meafures which the wifdom of our government may purfue to guard our national honor and protect our national rights, we are determined, with one heart, and one voice, to fupport them at the hazard of every domeftic confideration which may be near or dear to us ; and with an unfhaken confidence, we repofe our fafety and honor in the energy of your character, and the wifdom of your mind, as a ftatefman.

To the INHABITANTS *of the Town of* NEW-BERN.

GENTLEMEN,

AN addrefs fo cordial and refpectful as this from the citizens of Newbern, and your warm approbation of my conduct, fince I have filled the office of chief magiftrate of the United States, I ought to hold in the higheft eftimation.

I was indeed called to it at a crifis fraught with difficulty and danger ; when neither fkill in the management of affairs, more improved than any I could pretend to, nor the pureft integrity of intention, could fecure an an entire exemption from involuntary error, much less from censure.

There have been, for many years, strong indications that nothing would satisfy the rulers of the French, but our taking with them an active part in the war against all their enemies, and exhausting the last resources of our property to support them, not only in the pursuit of their chimerical ideas of liberty, but of universal empire: this we were not only under no obligation to do, but had reason to believe would have ruined the laws, constitution, and the morals of our country, as well as our credit and property.

An ardent enthusiasm, indeed, deluded for a long time too many of our worthy citizens.

The honor of your testimony to the integrity of my endeavors in so difficult a conjuncture, is very precious to my heart.

As the hostile views and nefarious designs of the French republic, are now too notorious to be denied or extenuated, I believe with you, that the love of our common country, will produce a cordial unanimity of sentiment.

This patriotic and spirited address is a clear indication of such desirable union, and will have a powerful tendency to encourage, strengthen and promote it.

JOHN ADAMS.

To JOHN ADAMS, President *of the* United States *of* America.

SIR,

WE, the inhabitants of the town of Wilmington, in the State of North-Carolina, legally convened together, feel it to be our incumbent duty to addrefs you at this very important crifis of the affairs of the United States in relation to the French republic.

Permit us to affure you, that we view with entire approbation the advances made by the executive authority of our own government to that of France, for an honorable and equitable adjuftment of all differences between the two republics.

We do not affect to conceal that from a feeming congeniality of fentiment refpecting civil liberty, and from the confideration that they were engaged with America in the conflict that terminated in her independence, we entertained a partiality and friendfhip for the people of France, fo long as the eftablifhment of a free and equal government appeared to be the virtuous object of their purfuit.

We lament, therefore, that thofe advances, inftead of being reciprocated in the manner that from their great candor and liberality, might reafonably have been expected, (and which for the interefts of both nations

nations was devoutly to be wiſhed) were repelled with indignity and contempt; and that it has become too evident, that principles replete with danger to this country, actuate the conduct of the preſent French government.

It muſt now be manifeſt to the world, that the unexampled moderation and forbearance of the government of the United States have ſerved only to excite to new aggreſſions on the part of France, and that no other alternative remains as a choice for the former, than conceſſion which would degrade our character as a nation, and ſap the foundation of its independency—or to reſort to thoſe defenſive meaſures which the ſpirit of the people and the reſources with which God has bleſſed us, enable us to call (and we truſt ſucceſsfully) into operation.

Appreciating the advantages of peace, and contraſting with them the calamities incidental to an oppoſite ſtate of things, we deprecate the approach of war; but ſtill we do not heſitate to declare, that if that extremity unavoidably becomes the final reſort, all the exertions that ſhould be expected in ſo juſt a cauſe, from men animated by an ardent love for their country, and reſolute to aſſert its rights and ſupport its government, may be depended on from us.

The

The annals of our country afford ample teſtimony of the zeal with which your talents and patriotiſm have been uniformly exerted in its ſervice ever ſince it aſſumed an independent ſituation. Your conduct in the diſcharge of the duties of the high ſtation you now fill, reflects new luſtre on your character, and dignity upon the government over which you preſide.

Thoroughly perſuaded, therefore, that it will be the great object of your adminiſtration to promote the ſafety, honor and proſperity of our common country, we humbly implore the bleſſing of the Supreme Being upon your endeavors, and that you may experience his peculiar care and providence.

To the INHABITANTS *of the Town of* WILMINGTON.

GENTLEMEN,

YOUR addreſs, unanimouſly adopted at a meeting legally convened, has been preſented to me by your ſenators in Congreſs, Mr. Martin and Mr. Bloodworth.

An aſſurance from the city of Wilmington, that you view with entire approbation, the advances made by the executive authority of your government to that of France, for an honorable and equitable adjuſtment of all differences between the two republics, is is of high value to me, and affords a convincing proof that Americans think and feel alike on great and essential objects, in all parts of the Union.

The friendship you entertained for the people of France, from a seeming congeniality of sentiment respecting civil liberty, and from the consideration that they were engaged with America in the conflict that terminated in our independence, so long as the establishment of a free and equal government appeared to be the virtuous object of their pursuit—far from being a reproach, was honorable to the disposition of your hearts.

The repulsion of our advances, candid, liberal and conciliatory, as all the impartial world will pronounce them, has indeed made it too evident, that principles replete with danger to this country, and to all others, actuate the conduct of the present French government.

It is also manifest to the world, that the unexampled moderation of America, has served only to excite new aggressions. Your declaration, that when the extremity of war becomes the final resort, all the exertions that should be exercised in so just a cause, from men animated by an ardent love of their country, and resolution to asserts its rights and support its government, may be depended upon—will be satisfactory to every

ery branch of the government, and highly pleasing to all your fellow-citizens.

The testimony of the citizens of Wilmington, to my zeal and industry in the public service, is very dear to me; and your petitions for the blessings of the Supreme Being on my endeavors, and that I may experience his peculiar care and providence, can be answered only by supplications on my part, for your country, yourselves, and your posterity.

JOHN ADAMS.

From the OFFICERS *of the* GUILFORD REGIMENT *of* MILITIA, *and the* INHABITANTS *of the County, to the* PRESIDENT *of the* UNITED STATES.

SIR,

AN address presented to you at this time, on the subject of the relative situation of America with foreign nations, but more particularly with France, should at least possess some novelty of thought to procure with you an apology, or some strong reason urged, why it had been so long delayed, to merit your reply. We hope you will not anticipate any thing new, for in fact, we only mean to adopt and urge the many and the excellent sentiments which have been already

ready addreſſed to you, by our fellow-citizens throughout the Union.

Loving our country, determined to ſupport it, its conſtitution, and the laws emanating from it; pleaſed with the adminiſtration of you, Sir, and your predeceſſor, who was and is no leſs beloved by you than by ourſelves; deteſting the parricidial principles of France, which not only ſeem, but really are ſubverting every government within their vortex;—can we be acquitted in our own minds? could we be in the opinion of our fellow-citizens, did we heſitate to make this declaration?

We abhor the modern innovations, and that word "*reform*," which in the fond credulity of our imaginations, we believed to be for the amelioration of the ſituation of man; we now ſhun it as we would a monſter ready to engulph all ſocial order, annihilate civil government, and ſubvert the heretofore approved courſe of things.

If France, compelled by that imperious neceſſity, which is ſometimes an apology with the hiſtorian, for acts tending to deſtroy a ſocial compact, could even produce that, an improper prejudice of America might ſtill furniſh her with apologiſts;---but when we ſee governments never yet obnoxious even to fanciful writers, as well as thoſe which imagination had formed tyrannical, and

and *our own*, which has for its basis every principle preservative of the happiness and security of virtue and industry, attempted to be destroyed;—can we resist the impulse of declaring that her nominal government is an unheard of tyranny---a compact which would as rapidly, and as effectually destroy our rising empire, as an army of their myrmidons might for the moment affect our internal order.

If we have not expressed these opinions so early as most of our fellow-citizens, receive, Sir, our apology;---so large an apportionment of the county of Guilford, never convened together as on this day, since the dispatches from our envoys to France, arrived, and delicacy of sentiment of those who did, prevented them from obtruding their opinions, as of those, who did not.

It is needless to tell you that your administration has our warmest approbation;—it is needless to tell you our determined resolution to support the measures of that administration; and it is only from your great and well-known goodness, we can hope an excuse for not expressing those opinions before this day.

We believe sincerely with you, Sir, in a sentiment lately expressed, that much indeed of our safety depends on the exertions used for the establishing an American navy, and that

that a part of our fellow-citizens cannot be more beneficially employed, than by endeavoring to perfect it.

May that kind Providence, which has watched over the liberty and independence of the United States, continue its protection to you, one of their choicest guardians, and long preserve a life dear and essential to its country's happiness.

To the OFFICERS *of the* GUILFORD REGIMENT *of* MILITIA, *and the* INHABITANTS *of the County.*

GENTLEMEN,

THE unanimous address adopted by you, has been transmitted as you directed, by Major John Hamilton to Mr. Steele, and by Mr. Steele to me.

Addresses like yours, so friendly to me and so animated with public spirit, can never stand in need of any apology. It is on the contrary, very true, that the affectionate addresses of my fellow-citizens have flowed in upon me from various parts of the Union, in such numbers, that it has been utterly impossible for me to preserve any regularity in my answers, without neglecting the indispensable duties of my office. This, and a long-continued and very dangerous sickness in my family, most seriously alarming to me, will,

will, I hope, be accepted by you and by all others whose favors have not been duly noticed, as an apology for a seeming neglect, which has been a very great mortification to me. There is no language within my command, sufficient to express the satisfaction I have felt, at the abundant proofs of harmony and unanimity among the people in the southern States, and in none more remarkably than in North-Carolina.

Your patriotic address, adopted on the ground where a memorable battle was fought by freemen, on the fifteenth of March, 1781, in defence of their liberties and independence, is peculiarly forcible and affecting.

JOHN ADAMS.

From the INHABITANTS *of* MOORE *County, to the* PRESIDENT *of the* UNITED STATES.

SIR,

THE present critical situation of America, with respect to foreign nations, calls upon its citizens as we conceive, to evince a spirit of harmony and unanimity among themselves; more especially at a juncture when it has artfully and maliciously been represented by our enemies that we are a divided people. We on our part have therefore thought it our duty openly to express our sentiments

sentiments on this subject; and to assure you as chief magistrate of our country, that we have entire confidence in its government; that we approve of the administration of our present Executive, particularly in its late endeavors to establish pacific measures with France; and that we are united, ready and determined, to oppose the machinations of that or any other foreign power, which shall attempt to invade our rights. In this we express the general sense of our county, and, we trust, of all America.

From the PEOPLE *of* CHAPEL HILL *and its vicinity, and the* YOUNG MEN *of the* UNIVERSITY, *to* JOHN ADAMS, PRESIDENT *of the* UNITED STATES.

SIR,

WE have long witnessed with deep concern, a disposition in the French government to abuse their power, in proportion as it has been increased. After it has grown, by a rapid and continued succession of victories, to a most extraordinary size, their profligacy and injustice are become no less extraordinary, and they have promiscuously confounded friends with foes in their piratical and predatory assaults. Had the barbarians themselves (for they have taught us the comparison) possessed the strength and means

means which that people have gained, we, with the reſt of the nations, muſt have expected to have our veſſels taken, our citizens ſtript of their property, our ſeamen abuſed and mercileſsly thrown into dungeons, or left to beg the neceſſaries of life. But could we ever have imagined, that France, a nation, but lately inferior to none in humanity of ſentiment, and refinement of manners, could ſo ſoon degenerate into barbariſm as to be guided by no law but power, or reſtrained by no conſiderations but thoſe of neceſſity? It is not without much ſurprize and regret, that we are at length forced to believe a nation capable of this ſhocking change in ſo ſhort a period. When we conſider how many others have been led on by the ſame example through the ſame change, we rejoice we yet feel ourſelves to have been in no great degree affected by its influence. We reflect with ſatisfaction, that the ſtrong chain of connexion that held us together at the commencement of their revolution, has not availed to drag our government and people into the ſame frightful gulf with themſelves, but that our eyes have been open to explore the courſe they were taking, and that in proportion as we have diſcovered the danger, we reſolved, and ſucceeded, to diſengage ourſelves.

It has not been without a ſtruggle in our boſoms, that we took ſo unpleaſing a reſolu-

tion;

tion; but when juſtice, religion and national independence muſt have been ſurrendered without it, we could no longer heſitate a moment.

Although our people have been divided in ſentiment even on this ſubject, as well as on others, yet when we are told that our differences are made a ground on which to form a plan for deſtroying our government, or infringing our rights, we cannot but revolt at the ungenerous thought, and execrate the man who could think of acting on ſo baſe a principle.

It is to convince you, Sir, and the enemies who have calculated on ſo inſidious a ſcheme of the miſtake they are in, and the ſevere diſappointment they are likely to ſuffer ſhould they further proceed upon it, that we undertake thus publicly to addreſs you. And although it is thus late that we have done it, we truſt that it is with no leſs ſincerity, than others who have preceded us. Whatever political diſagreement may have ſubſiſted among us, or however unfortunate they may have been in their effects, we ſhall never harbor the ignoble thought of ſacrificing our country, our government, or its adminiſtration, to the accompliſhment of local or perſonal views. After the proofs we had given of our inſuperable love of independence, in our ſtruggle againſt Britain, none but thoſe who had experienced in themselves a most unaccountable degeneracy, could have imagined we should be willing so soon to renounce it for the sake of retaining the favor, or promoting the views of any other nation under heaven. But when we consider the wanton and unprecedented conduct of the Directory in setting at nought the ordinary laws of nations, and assuming to create a new code fitted to their own purposes of plunder and violence; when we reflect on their unworthy treatment of our ambassadors, and the unexampled insults they have returned for all the anxiety which you, Sir, in conjunction with our government, have manifested for peace and justice, we can no longer remain silent spectators: We feel it our indispensable duty to declare, that we have an unimpaired confidence in your wisdom and administration; that we feel an attachment to your person as our chief magistrate, and one who has borne a distinguished part in the defence and establishment of our rights and liberties—and that when those liberties and rights are placed at stake, we are ready to stand by you and our government, to defend both at the expense of our last blood.

We cannot but consider our commerce, and that worthy class of our fellow-citizens who are employed in it, as entitled to the same protection with ourselves. It would be blindness in us not to perceive the merit of of that part of society, who brave the dangers and hardships of the ocean, to supply us with what we should with the utmost difficulty and disadvantage, provide for ourselves, and which we have a perfect right to obtain without molestation, by a fair and honest commerce with all who are willing to trade with us.

SOUTH-CAROLINA.

The ADDRESS *and* MEMORIAL *of the* CITIZENS *of* CHARLESTON, *to* JOHN ADAMS, PRESIDENT *of the* UNITED STATES,—

SHEWETH RESPECTFULLY,

THAT your memorialists learnt, with the most sincere satisfaction, the appointment, by the executive government of the United States, of a solemn embassy, duly empowered and wisely instructed, to endeavor to remove all differences with the French republic, and to maintain the relations of amity and peace between the two countries.

That your memorialists have understood with the deepest regret, that the spirit of conciliation and peace manifested by the government of the United States, hath been met by a spirit of hostility in the councils of the French republic; and that the ministers of peace

peace had not been admitted to the privilege of an audience, ſcarcely ever denied among civilized nations.

That the moſt unreaſonable demands have been made upon this country, by perſons pretending and appearing to act under the authority of the French government, (but which, it is ſincerely hoped, not with the ſentiments of the people of France) without even the pretence of injury or wrong having been committed—demands which, if ſubmitted to, would proſtrate the United States at the feet of France, and convert her from a free and independent nation, into a tributary and degraded province.

Your memorialiſts are aſtoniſhed to find that theſe demands have been perſeveringly urged, upon a preſumption that the Americans were a divided people, and would never unite in ſupport of their own government, in oppoſition to theſe demands; and that upon this fallacious idea, our commerce hath been harraſſed, without redreſs; and our peace and our independence are threatened.

Deeply afflicted at this ſtate of the public affairs, your memorialiſts feel themſelves irreſiſtibly impelled to make a full, ſolemn and explicit declaration of their ſincere attachment to the conſtitution and government of the United States; and of their fixed reſolution to maintain and ſupport them againſt

all

all foreign encroachment and dominion, at the hazard of their lives and fortunes.—Your memorialists are but too well acquainted with the miseries and calamities of war, and they would willingly have averted them by the sacrifice of secondary interests. But they do not hesitate to declare their preference of every calamity to a servile subjection to a foreign yoke.

Your memorialists repose confidence in the wisdom and patriotism of the constituted authorities; and trust that the most prompt, vigorous and efficacious steps will be taken, "to provide for the common defence, promote the general welfare, and secure the blessings of liberty to ourselves and our posterity;" and they submit, to the discretion of the government, the measures essential to the attainment and security of these great objects.

From the INHABITANTS *of* CLARMONT *County, to the* PRESIDENT, SENATE, *and House of* REPRESENTATIVES *of the* UNITED STATES.

GENTLEMEN,

WHEN our peace and independence is menaced by a formidable though perfidious nation, who, aspiring to the domination of the world, violates, in the career of her ambition, all bonds of good faith, and all ties of that friendship which heretofore happily ſubſiſted between that nation and our own,—we think it not improper in us, nor diſagreeable to you, that we come forward under an open avowal of the ſentiments which actuate us at this momentous criſis.

Deeply impreſſed with a ſenſe of your wiſdom and patriotiſm, and cordially approving of the pacific meaſures you have taken to effect a reconciliation and an amicable adjuſtment of the differences between the two nations, we cannot but feel an indignation, worthy the breaſts of freemen, at ſeeing thoſe meaſures rejected with haughty contempt by the French government. And notwithſtanding we deprecate the calamities of war, yet we view them as but a ſecondary conſideration compared with the degradation of our national dignity, and the ſubverſion of our government.

Relying firmly on the wiſdom and fidelity of the conſtituted authorities of the United States, we do not heſitate to declare, that we will ſupport, at the riſk of our lives and fortunes, any meaſures that they may think proper to adopt for the defence of our country's rights; and that we will evince to the world we are not a divided people.

To the PRESIDENT *of the* UNITED STATES.

SIR,

THE inhabitants of the town of Cambridge and its vicinity, in the diſtrict of Ninety-Six,

Ninety-Six, and State of South-Carolina, having aſſembled for the purpoſe of taking into conſideration the political ſtate of our own country, beg leave to ſtate to you, as chief magiſtrate of the United States, our ſincere regret, that, from preſent appearances, we are likely to be involved in the war, which for years paſt, has deſolated a conſiderable part of Europe. Although as citizens, we hold ſacred the right of judging of the conduct and meaſures of our rulers, and expreſſing freely and publicly our opinions thereon, yet we ſhall always view with a jealous eye, and will repel, with the energy of republicans, (who have fought for, and of courſe know the value of genuine liberty) the attempts of any foreign nation, who may ſhew a diſpoſition to interfere in the councils of our country. We therefore beg leave, through you, to aſſure our fellow-citizens throughout the Union, that although agricultural in our habits, and attached to the paths of peace, we are, to a man, united to defend our country from the unjuſt aggreſſion of any foreign power, and prepared, with our lives and fortunes, to defend the conſtitution and independence of our country, and to ſupport its officers in the conſtitutional and legitimate exerciſe of all their functions.

GEORGIA.

GEORGIA.

To JOHN ADAMS, PRESIDENT *of the* UNITED STATES.

SIR,

THE inhabitants of the city of Savannah and its vicinity, impreſſed with the value of national independence, and of the wiſdom and virtue which have characterized a government ſo happily calculated to enſure and preſerve this bleſſing, cannot withhold their approbation to the meaſures which you have purſued at a juncture ſo critical to the United States, as the preſent.

Fondly anticipating the reſtoration of a good underſtanding on principles compatible with juſtice and honor, with a nation for whom America had always manifeſted ſentiments of the moſt real and undiſguiſed friendſhip, they ſaw with pleaſure the departure of the commiſſioners entruſted with this object, whoſe perſonal characters juſtified an entire confidence (and which the event has proved not to have been miſplaced) that no ſuitable means would be neglected in purſuing the important object of their miſſion. And notwithſtanding the painful and inexpreſſible ſenſation which the conduct of men, at the head of a government once our allies and friends, excited, there remains a conſolation,

consolation, that the cause and responsibility of this conduct will rest on themselves alone. And it is with great pleasure that we congratulate you, Sir, and our country on the wise and prudent measures you have pursued for the preservation of peace and the protection of our independence; we believe that you have done as much for the obtainment of the first of these objects, as a due regard for the other would justify or permit; —and should the last argument of nations, a resort to arms, become indispensable for the protection of those rights which are the most dear to us—we pledge ourselves for the support of our government, by which alone they can be secured, and at the hazard of our lives and properties, to convince the world that we will take no share in the disgrace of being considered a divided people.

To JOHN ADAMS, PRESIDENT *of the* UNITED STATES.

SIR,

A MEETING of the inhabitants of the town of Washington and county of Wilkes, in the State of Georgia, having delegated to us, as a committee, the power of addressing in their names the chief executive magistrate of the Union on the present situation of public affairs as they relate to foreign nations, we we embrace the earliest opportunity to discharge the trust so reposed in us.

Whilst we cannot but deplore the present prospect of national calamity, and anticipate with sensibility the deep distress which must be common in our country should that prospect be realized, we should at the same time express to you, sentiments the reverse of those which universally pervade this part of the community, were we not to attribute the impending evils to the injustice of those with whom we are connected by public ties. To the constant endeavors of the American government for the maintenance of its neutrality, have been opposed the intrigues of foreign courts to involve it in the labyrinth of European wars.—To unremitted and sincere exertions for the preservation of peace and the cultivation of harmony, have been opposed unwarranted encroachments on our most sacred rights, and studied indignity to our applications for reparation.

Foreign nations have represented the Americans to be a divided people. Were we in reality so, their conduct would not fail to unite us;—and should any daring invader on the common rights of human nature presume to enforce its unjust purposes by public force, experience will then teach them they have been deceived.

Although

Although we are here ſurrounded—on one ſide by powerful ſavage tribes, among whom the intrigues of foreign agents are generally too ſucceſsful; bounded on another by the territories of a nation apparently not altogether friendly; and open on a third to the approaches of the weakeſt naval armaments; yet, Sir, the people of this country feel no diſpoſition to ſubmit with tameneſs to outrages upon common juſtice, and inſults upon public and individual honor. They view with indignation the unprecedented violations of national rights committed by thoſe to whom the American government have aſſiduouſly held out the olive branch of peace.—They feel the ſtrongeſt emotions of reſentment for the ſhameful demands made, as terms upon which our public miniſters might obtain the privilege of repreſenting our grievances. With an acquieſcence in ſuch requiſitions, may the American character never be tarniſhed.

We cannot forego the preſent occaſion to declare the grateful ſenſe we entertain for the anxiety manifeſted by the federal Executive for the proſperity of our common country, and the preſervation of our general happineſs. The citizens of our community cannot but applaud that ſpirit of moderation which prompted the American government, after repeated indignities, to make a laſt ſtruggle for amicable accommodation of

exiſting

existing differences. Notwithstanding more has been done than could have been justified by any other principle, than that of an ardent and sincere desire for the preservation of peace, the prospect has with every step become more gloomy. Our solicitudes and our concessions have added insults to injury. To concede farther, would render us a degraded people—to ask more from those who have set at defiance the acknowledged principles of national justice and national honor, would render us undeserving of the respect of all mankind.

Under these impressions, we are prepared for the worst. Through you, Sir, as the chief organ of our country, we beg leave to express our confidence in the constituted authorities of the government. Be assured that the people of this part of the community are impressed with a firm determination to resist any encroachments which may have for their object, either an interference with the sovereignty of our country, or an aggression upon our public or individual rights. And the government of the United States will receive our most decided support to any measures which may be adopted for the maintenance of our national honor, and the preservation of our independence.

GENERAL WASHINGTON's LETTER *to* PRESIDENT ADAMS, *on his* APPOINTMENT *to the Office of* COMMANDER IN CHIEF OF ALL THE ARMIES OF THE UNITED STATES.

Mount Vernon, 13th July, 1798.

DEAR SIR,

I HAD the honor on the evening of the 11th instant, to receive from the hand of the Secretary of War, your favor of the 7th, announcing that you had, with the advice and consent of the Senate, appointed me "Lieutenant-General and Commander in Chief of all the Armies raised, or to be raised, for the service of the United States."

I cannot express how greatly affected I am at this new proof of public confidence, and the highly flattering manner in which you have been pleased to make the communication; at the same time I must not conceal from you my earnest wish, that the choice had fallen upon a man less declined in years, and better qualified to encounter the usual vicissitudes of war.

You know, Sir, what calculation I had made relative to the probable course of events, on my retiring from office, and the

 determination

determination I had consoled myself with, of closing the remnant of my days in my present peaceful abode; you will therefore be at no loss to conceive and appreciate the sensations I must have experienced, to bring my mind to any conclusion that would pledge me, at so late a period of life, to leave scenes I sincerely love, to enter upon the boundless field of public action, incessant trouble, and high responsibility.

It was not possible for me to remain ignorant of, or indifferent to, recent transactions. The conduct of the Directory of France towards our country; their insidious hostility to its government; their various practices to withdraw the affections of the people from it; the evident tendency of their acts and those of their agents to countenance and invigorate opposition; their disregard of solemn treaties and the laws of nations; their war upon our defenceless commerce; their treatment of our ministers of peace; and their demands amounting to tribute;—could not fail to excite in me corresponding sentiments with those my countrymen have so generally expressed in their affectionate addresses to you. Believe me, Sir, no one can more cordially approve of the wise and prudent measures of your administration. They ought to inspire universal confidence, and will, no doubt, combined

with

with the ſtate of things, call from Congreſs ſuch laws and means as will enable you to meet the full force and extent of the criſis.

Satisfied, therefore, that you have ſincerely wiſhed and endeavored to avert war, and exhauſted to the laſt drop, the cup of reconciliation, we can with pure hearts appeal to Heaven for the juſtice of our cauſe; and may confidently truſt the final reſult to that kind Providence who has heretofore, and ſo often, ſignally favored the people of theſe United States.

Thinking in this manner, and feeling how incumbent it is upon every perſon, of every deſcription, to contribute at all times to his country's welfare, and eſpecially in a moment like the preſent, when every thing we hold dear and ſacred is ſo ſeriouſly threatened; I have finally determined to accept the commiſſion of Commander in Chief of the Armies of the United States; with the reſerve only, that I ſhall not be called into the field until the army is in a ſituation to require my preſence, or it becomes indiſpenſable by the urgency of circumſtances.

In making this reſervation, I beg it to be underſtood, that I do not mean to withhold any aſſiſtance to arrange and organize the army, which you may think I can afford. I take the liberty alſo to mention, that I muſt decline having my acceptance conſidered as

drawing

drawing after it any immediate charge upon the public; or that I can receive any emoluments annexed to the appointment, before entering into a situation to incur expense.

The Secretary of War being anxious to return to the seat of government, I have detained him no longer than was necessary to a full communication upon the several points he had in charge.

With very great respect and consideration,

I have the honor to be,

Dear Sir,

Your most obedient humble servant,

G. WASHINGTON.

JOHN ADAMS,
President of the United States.

THE END.

INDEX.

Ff 2 DISTRICT

Of

DELAWARE.

MARYLAND.

VIRGINIA.

Of

NORTH-CAROLINA.

SOUTH-CAROLINA.

GEORGIA.

SUBSCRIBERS' NAMES.

[If there are any omiſſions of titles, &c. or other errors in the following liſt of ſubſcribers' names, it is requeſted they may be excuſed, and attributed to want of ſufficient information.]

A

GEN. STEPHEN ABBOT, Salem.
Z. B. Adams, Eſq. Charleſtown.
Daniel Auſtin, ditto.
John Auſtin, do.
N. Auſtin, jun. do.
Nathan Adams, do.
Dr. Iſaac Adams, Newb. Port.
Rev. John Andrews, ditto.
Eli Adams, Dublin, (N. H.)
Benjamin Adams, jun. Rowley.
Benjamin Alline, Boſton.
R. G. Amory, Eſq. ditto.
C. W. Apthorp, do.
Richard Auſtin, do.

B

Dr. J. Bartlett, Charleſtown.
George Bartlett, ditto.
Samuel Bradſtreet, do.
John Breed, do.
Eben. Baker, Boſton.
G. L. Barrett, ditto.
Thomas Bartlett, do.
Daniel Bowen, do.
Solomon Blake, do.
Samuel Brewer, do.
Jonathan Balch, jun. do.
Robert Breck, jun. do.
Samuel Bradford, do.
Francis Brinley, do.
Aſa Bullard, do.
William Bartlett, Newb. Port.
Edmund Bartlett, 2 cop. ditto.
Stephen Bartlett, do.
Edward Baſs, *Biſhop*, do.
Rev. John Boddily, do.
Peter L. Briton, do.
Hon. Theoph. Bradbury, do.
Capt. Moſes Brown, 2 cop. do.
Moſes Brown, do.
Samuel Brown, Newb. Port.
Daniel Burnham, ditto.
Wm. Biglow, A. M. Salem.
Rev. T. Barnard, D. D. ditto.
John Biſhop, Medford.
Gen. J. Brooks, ditto.
Rev. Iſaac Braman, Rowley.
Dr. John Bartlett, Roxbury.
Thomas Beede, A. B. ditto.
Jeremiah S. Boies, Eſq. Milton.

C

Joſeph Cabot, A. M. Salem.
Capt. Benj. Carpenter, ditto.
Thomas C. Cuſhing, do.
John St. Capt, Boſton.
Joſeph Callender, 2 cop. ditto.
Samuel Clarke, do.
William Cochran, do.
John Coe, do.
William Crafts, 2 cop. do.
Allen Crocker, do.
R. Crocker, do.
George A. Cuſhing, do.
Rev. Thomas Cary, Newb. Port.
Thomas Cary, jun. A. B. ditto.
Capt. Ebenezer Choate, do.
Triſtram Coffin, do.
David Coffin, do.
Philip Coombs, do.
William Coombs, do.
A. Childs, Charleſtown.

D

William Dall, Boſton.
Hon. John Davis, ditto.
S. Dillaway, do.
Weare Dow, do.
Robert Duncan, jun. do.
George W. Duncan, do.
Charles Davis, 2 cop. Roxbury.
Rev. Daniel Dana, Newb. Port.

Elias H. Derby, Esq. Salem.
Elias H. Derby, jun. Esq. ditto.
E. H. Derby, A. M. do.
Benjamin Dodge, do.
George Dodge, do.
John Dutch, jun. do.
James Derby, Medford.
Hon. Samuel Dexter, Charlestown, 3 copies.

E

Henry Edes, Boston.
Ephraim Emerson, Salem.

F

Jona. Fay, Esq. 6 cop. Concord.
Samuel P. Fay, A. B. ditto.
Dr. Nahum Fay, Boston.
Ebenezer Failey, ditto
William Fisk, do.
Capt. Simon Forrester, Salem.
Samuel Foster, Newb. Port.
Moses Frazier, ditto
Andrew Frothingham, do.
Theodore D. Foster, Providence.

G

His Honor Moses Gill, Princeton, 3 copies.
Jonathan Gage, Newb. Port.
Hon. Jona. Greenleaf, ditto.
Joshua Greenleaf, do.
John Greenleaf, do.
Jacob Gates, Boston.
John Gardner, ditto.
Edward Gray, Esq. do.
Samuel L. Green, do.
Henry Gardner, Salem.
Samuel Gray, ditto
William Gray, jun. do.
William Gray, tertius, do.
Hon. B. Goodhue, do.
S. Gorham, jun. Charlestown.
David Gloyd, 6 cop. Abbington,

H

Capt. Eben. Hale, Newb. Port.
James Hodge, ditto.
Thomas W. Hooper, do.
Michael Hodge, Newb. Port.
Capt. Stephen Howard, ditto.
Elias Hunt, do.
Joseph P. Hall, Medford.
Gilbert Hall, ditto.
J. Hall, Boston.
Dr. Lemuel Hayward, ditto.
Jonathan Harris, do.
John Heard, A. M. do.
Stephen Higginson, do.
Henry Hill, do.
John Houghton, do.
James Hughes, Esq. do.
Thomas Hartshorn, Esq. Salem.
John Harthorn, jun. A. B. ditto.
Joseph Hiller, Esq. do.
Capt. Benj. Hodges, do.
Dr. Ed. A. Holyoke, do.
Rev. T. M. Harris, Dorchester.
Thomas Heald, A. M. Concord.
Dr. Abiel Heywood, ditto.
Dr. Joseph Hunt, do.
Dr. Isaac Hurd, do.
Jona. P. Hitchcock, Brookfield.
Oliver Holden, Charlestown.
Benjamin Hurd, jun. ditto.
Joseph Hurd, do.
Joseph Hurd, jun. A. B. do.
James Howe, Roxbury.

I

Capt. John Ingersoll, Salem.
Capt. J. Ingraham, Cambridge, 2 copies.

J

James Jackson, A. B. Salem.
John Jenks, ditto.
Daniel Jenks, do.
James Jeffrey, do.
Edward Jackson, Boston.
Patrick Jackson, Newb. Port.
Wm. P. Johnson, ditto.
Capt. Eleazer Johnson, do.
Capt. W. Jones, Concord.
Thomas Johnston, Charlestown.

K

Rev. Joseph M'Kean, Milton.

Thomas Kettell, Charlestown.
James King, Salem.
Rev. John T. Kirkland, Boston.
Joseph Knapp, ditto.
Wm. Kempton, do.
Caleb Kimball, Newb. Port.
Capt. Anthony Knapp. ditto.
Capt. William Knapp, do.

L

Capt. George Lane, Charlestown, 2 copies.
Deacon John Larkin, ditto.
Thomas O. Larkin, do.
William Lewis, do.
Jonathan Lambert, Salem.
Capt. Abel Laurence, ditto.
Moses Little, do.
William Lang, do.
Edward J. Lang, jun, do.
Peter Lander, do.
Michael Little, Newb. Port.
Deacon Robert Long, ditto.
Nathaniel Lord, A. B. Ipswich.
Hon. John Lowell, Roxbury, 3 copies.

M

Col. Sabin Mann, Medford.
Jonathan March, Newb. Port.
Hugh Mowatt, ditto.
Rev. Charles W. Milton, do.
Daniel Mason, Chelsea.
Capt. W. Marston, Salem.
John Murphy, Salem.
Samuel Miller, Boston
Rev. John Murray, ditto.
Rev. J. Morse, D. D. Charlestown, 3 copies.

N

Henry Newman, Esq. Boston.
Capt. W. M'Neil, ter. Charlestown.
Jeremiah Nelson, Newb. Port.
Dr. Bishop Norton, ditto.
Capt. William Noyes, do.
Ichabod Nichols, Salem.
John Norris, Esq. Salem.
Abijah Northey, jun. ditto.

O

Edward Oliver, Boston.
Francis J. Oliver, A. M. ditto.
Dr. B. L. Oliver, Salem.
Isaac Osgood, Esq. ditto.
Joseph Osgood, do.
Nathl. G. Olney, Providence.
Samuel A. Otis, Newb. Port.

P

Thomas Paine, Boston.
Thomas Paine, A. M. ditto.
Joseph Pope, do.
Benjamin Proctor, do.
Samuel Parkman, do.
Ralph Pope, do.
Joseph Powell, do.
John Page, Salem.
Joseph Perkins, Esq. ditto.
Benjamin Pickman, Esq. do.
Benj. Pickman, jun. Esq. do.
Dudley L. Pickman, do.
Benjamin Pierce, do.
Nathan Pierce, do.
Robert Peele, do.
William Prescott, Esq. do.
Edward Pulling, Esq. do.
Samuel Putnam, Esq. do.
John Punchard, do.
Aaron Pardee, Newb. Port.
Amos Pearson, ditto.
Richard Pike, do.
Daniel Parker, Charlestown, 2 copies.
John Phillips, A. M. ditto.
E. Porter, Roxbury.

R

Dr. Isaac Rand, Boston.
Dr. Isaac Rand, jun. ditto.
Joseph Richards, do.
William Richardson, do.
Edward Rand, Newb. Port.
Samuel Richardson, ditto.
Capt. John Rogers, do.

John Richardson, Concord.
Nathaniel J. Robbins, Milton.
Brackly Rose, Salem.
John M. Russell, Esq. Charlestown, 2 copies.

S.

His Excellency INCREASE SUMNER, 2 cop. Roxbury.
John Swift, ditto.
Josiah Salisbury, A. B. Boston.
David Sears, Esq. ditto.
Thomas O. Selfridge, A.B. do.
John C. Shindle, do.
Holder Slocum, jun. do.
William Stone, do.
Richard Sullivan, A. B. do.
Jesse Sumner, do.
Charles P. Sumner, A. B. do.
Samuel Swift, do.
Jacob Saunderson, Salem.
Richard Smith, ditto.
Joseph Sprague, do.
Artemas Sawyer, A.B. Lancaster.
F. Sisson, Charlestown.
Capt. Daniel Scott, ditto.
Capt. James Smith, Cambridge.
Leonard Smith, Newb. Port.
John Smith, ditto.
Rev. Samuel Spring, do.
Eben. Stocker, do.
Amos Spofford, Rowley.

T.

Samuel Toppan, Newb. Port.
William Titcomb, ditto.
Gen. Jonathan Titcomb, do.
Deac. Thomas Thompson, do.
Benjamin Thurston, do.
Nicholas Tracy, do.
Stephen Tilton, do.
Enoch Titcomb, do.
Benjamin Tucker, do.
E. Tufts, do.
Dudley A. Tyng, Esq. do.
Fitch Tarbett, Medford.
Hall Tufts, A. M. ditto.
Capt. Nathaniel Thayer, Boston.
Stephen Thayer, ditto.
Abraham Tuckerman, do.
Edward Tuckerman, jun. do.
George W. Tuckerman, do.
James Temple, A.M. Concord.
Capt. Gideon Tucker, Salem.

V.

Joseph Vincent, Salem.

W.

Capt. T. Walker, Charlestown.
Col. David Wood, ditto.
Aaron Wait, Salem.
Jonathan Waldo, ditto.
Joshua Ward, do.
William Ward, do.
Capt. Edward West, do.
Michael Walsh, Newb. Port.
Eben. Wheelwright, ditto.
Gilman White, do.
David Wood, do.
Capt. William Wyer, do.
N. Wyer, do.
J. Waters, jun. Boston.
Rev. Wm. Walter, D. D. ditto, 2 copies.
Robert Wyer, A. M. do.
Nathan Webb, do.
Nath. P. West, do.
Abraham Wild, do.
Dr. Joseph Whipple, do.
Benjamin White, do.
Nathaniel Whitwell, do.
William Whitwell, do.
Conrade Webb, A. B. Virginia.
Deacon John White, Concord, 6 copies.
Stephen Wood, ditto.
D. A. White, A. M. Medford.
William H. Williams, Providence, (R. I.)
Thomas Williams, Esq. Roxbury, 2 copies.
John Williams, Esq.
William Wyer, Beverly.

www.ingramcontent.com/pod-product-compliance
Lightning Source LLC
Chambersburg PA
CBHW021105270326
41929CB00009B/743
9783337192365